on the
CHILE trail

on the
CHILE trail

100 Great Recipes from Across America

coyote joe

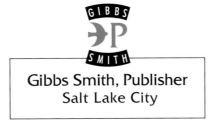

Gibbs Smith, Publisher
Salt Lake City

First Edition
09 08 07 06 05   5 4 3 2 1

Published by
Gibbs Smith, Publisher
P.O. Box 667
Layton, Utah 84041

1.800.748.5439 orders
www.gibbs-smith.com

Designed and produced by Dawn DeVries Sokol
Printed and bound in China

Library of Congress Cataloging-in-Publication Data

Coyote Joe.
On the chile trail / Coyote Joe.— 1st ed.
p. cm.
Includes index.
ISBN 1-58685-404-6
1. Cookery (Hot peppers) 2. Hot peppers. I. Title.
TX803.P46M34 2005
641.6'384—dc22
          2004021363

When I was first married, my father had me read an article that likened a career path with a horse race. The idea being, choose the winner and then get directly behind him. Stay close and try to pass him at the finish line. This has served me well.

I dedicate this book to the four horsemen of my career:

To Paul Elswick, who slowly and with some trouble taught me the rules of writing. Paul convinced me to start writing in the first place. My friend is no longer with us and I miss him greatly.

To Bruce Jones, the television producer who explained that all I needed to do was be myself and he would make it work in post. Bruce is a dear friend; his sense of humor and timing is impeccable.

To Dave DeWitt, who has answered every question I've ever had about chiles and the hot and spicy food business. Dave is not only the world's leading authority on chiles, he serves as "The Godfather" for the entire industry.

And last but certainly not least, to my "amigo," Bob Boze Bell. For twenty years Bob has helped me at every corner. He has encouraged and believed in me. And always found the time to help me with career decisions and direction.

CONTENTS

CATHOLICS

COWBOYS

CALIFORNIANS 135

ACKNOWLEDGMENTS

I'd like to start by thanking the two people whom I always turn to when a flavor or food problem evades me.

First my wife, old friend, and cooking partner, Chef Kathy. She always adds that little twist that takes my cooking over the top. When I'm acting like a man rushing off to a meeting looking for his socks, Kathy always knows where to look for that flavor I need but can't put my finger on.

And next, Ritchie Fliegler, my brother in food. This guy is who I would have been (culinarily speaking) if I had been raised in Brooklyn. Whenever I have a question about any foods from New York or the East Coast in general, I call Ritchie. He once gave me a forty-five minute lecture on the difference between a New York and Chicago-style hot dog, complete with ordering instructions so the street vendor doesn't think I'm a tourist. In short, when it comes to food Ritchie gets it!

INTRODUCTION

OUR STORY BEGINS FIVE HUNDRED YEARS AGO with Columbus landing in the New World on the island of Hispaniola. The Queen of Spain has financed the trip and wants a return on her investment. Among other things, she wants gold, silver, and spices. The most expensive spice in the world at the time is black pepper, reportedly worth its weight in silver. Columbus finds a little gold and a little silver, but not enough. He is badly in need of a treasure to send back to the queen.

There are several varieties of little bright-red seedpods that the natives use to spice up their diet. They call them *chile,* which is the Nuatal, or Aztec, word for *sharp.* The native peoples of Central and South America have been eating and cultivating chiles for thousands of years. Chiles are so ingrained in their societies that they are eaten with virtually every meal and are worshiped as part of native creation mythology. One explorer in the expedition wrote in his journal, "The Indians eat that fruit [chiles] like we eat apples."

As a way out of his troubles, Columbus decides that these little fireballs are in fact a new variety of black pepper. He bastardizes the two words, *chile* and *pimienta*, or "pepper" in English, creating "chile pepper." Chiles are not peppers and are in no way related to their new namesake—black pepper.

Chiles are a New World food. That's right. Before Columbus, no chiles in Europe, Asia, Africa, Australia, and on down the list. Good ol' Chris sends the seeds back to Spain, where they are quickly cultivated and then sold around the world. The wild varieties

the original plant. The cycle continues. After twenty or thirty decades there are chile plants growing, cross-pollinating, and creating new varieties all over the world.

Today, for those of us who love chile peppers, life simply would not be the same without them. Let's face it: they have worked their way into the culinary fabric of the USA. During the past forty years in this country, consumption of hot and spicy foods has multiplied exponentially. Devotees, or "chile heads" as they are better known, are so fanatical about the pungent pods that there are now two national magazines devoted to mouth-burning cuisine. Salsa and hot sauce outsell barbecue sauce, ketchup, and mus-

For those of us who love chile peppers, life simply would not be the same without them.

growing in the jungles of Africa and Asia are the result of a process known as "bird propagation." A bird eats the chiles growing in a garden and flies away. The seeds (along with a little fertilizer) pass through the bird, and soon a new chile plant pops up miles from

tard combined. The national appetite for increasingly hotter foods is so strong that even the fast-food giants are jumping on the bandwagon by including several items on their menus that run the heat gamut from mild to wild. This is not some passing phase; we have become a chile-pepper-loving nation!

And what about that heat? The main concentration is found in the white flesh and veins in the center of the chiles. The seed's heat is caused by proximity with this flesh, which actually generates the heat. So when trying to *chilly, chille, chiley, chilley, chile,* and *chili.* At this point, the accepted spelling for the fruit of our favorite plant and the resulting green and red stew made in Mexico, Arizona, California, and New Mexico is C-H-I-L-E. The word *chili* is the correct spelling for that wonderful dish from Texas—chili con carne.

There are five separate regions within the Chile Belt.

reduce the heat level in a recipe, remove the seedpod, any loose seeds, and all the veins. A chemical substance known as capsaicin causes the burning sensation we've all come to love. It irritates pain receptors in the mouth, nose, and throat. This irritation causes the brain to produce endorphins, which in turn produce a sense of well-being. This sensation, by the way, is similar to the effects of morphine. That is why we still reach for another chip full of burning-hot salsa when our mouths are on fire. Going back time and again to this blissful but painful experience is so common that it has been given a name: mouth surfing.

There is a long history of different spellings for the red-hot fruit of the gods. I have seen

In the following pages we will take a lip-burning, forehead-sweating, back-road trip through a part of America that runs from eastern Louisiana to the California coast—the Chile Belt. There are five separate regions within the Chile Belt. They have individually affected the eating habits of the country and even the world. We'll stop by each for a little visit, see the sights, hear the stories, and taste the amazing tongue-tingling local favorites. Along the way, we'll learn how each cuisine has developed and which chile peppers help define that region. So, bring along your appetite, hold on to your taste buds, and saddle up. It's time to head out . . . on the chile trail!

CAJUNS

IN MY LATE TWENTIES I HAD MY FIRST TASTE OF CAJUN COOKING.

It knocked my socks off . . . a whole new world of hot and spicy flavors! Later, when I discovered the differences between Cajun and Creole, that world was once again expanded. Prior to that time, most of my chile-eating experience was based in Mexican food. But what I found in the cuisine of Louisiana was a different equation, a regional blending of chiles with old-world French and local influences. The flavors were sharply defined. In this chapter we'll taste a wide variety of the famous dishes from this region. If you're new to Cajun and Creole or have only tried a "blackened" whatever at the local diner, get ready for a red-hot, mind-blowing experience. Let me tell you how these foods were developed before we get cooking.

In 1785 the British government forced about six hundred French settlers, known as Acadians, from their homelands in Nova Scotia. Because there were French already living throughout Louisiana, many Acadians settled in the swamps and woods there. They were poor farmers, trappers, fishermen, and hunters. The local natives mispronounced *Acadian* as "Cagian," which later became "Cajun." There's an old saying that goes something like this: If it crawls, walks, swims, or slithers a Cajun will eat it! But this can be said for those of limited means worldwide. Struggling people can't afford to waste anything, least of all food. This is where culinary magic happens. People in a tight situation figure out how to use a food source that is fairly abundant where they live. Through trial and error they find ways to make it more palat-

able and share the recipe with friends and family. These recipes are then handed down through generations, each one adding its own twist. Over time, what was once bland sustenance develops into a regional favorite that is downright delicious.

Someone who has witnessed this process firsthand is world-famous chef Paul Prudhomme. This guy is pure Cajun. He was born in Opelousas, Louisiana, the youngest of ten brothers and three sisters. His dad was a poor sharecropper who grew sweet potatoes and cotton. In Paul's famous book *The Louisiana Kitchen,* he tells of his father spending forty-two years working behind a pair of mules. Paul was only seven when his last sister got married and moved away. This meant a promotion to the kitchen for young Paul. It was hard work, but he developed a feel for the land and picked up a good working knowledge of cooking from his mother. That knowledge served him well in years to come. At seventeen Paul officially started his cooking career; he went on the road for twelve years, looking for any cooking job where he could pick up cooking techniques, especially ethnic. The problem he ran into time and again was, he often found himself the teacher! At that time not many folks outside of Louisiana knew about spicy Creole or flaming-hot Cajun cooking. Everywhere he went this new cuisine was an instant hit. Around age thirty he went back home, believing that Louisiana was the culinary center of the universe. From 1975 to 1980 he served as corporate chef for the New Orleans landmark Brennan's.

1980s Cajun food invasion that swept the country.

Cajun cooking is often thrown in with Creole. The Creole were already established when the Cajun showed up on the scene. In the 1700s the Spanish who were governing the area in and around New Orleans gave the name "Criollo" to any person of European descent. The name, which later became "Creole," stood for those of the upper crust—those who were refined, cultured, and well bred. The resulting cuisine was "old-world French meets the flavors of the Caribbean islands," influenced by the

Cajun cooking is often thrown in with Creole.

From 1980 to the present he has operated K-Paul's with his wife and partner Kay Hinrichs. *National Restaurant News* says K-Paul's is one of the ten best restaurants in the world. Paul Prudhomme is the embodiment of this regional cooking and is single-handedly responsible for the

Spanish and Africans living in the area. Creole cooking, known for its use of butter, cream, and tomatoes, is considered a type of "fine dining." Both Creole and Cajun cuisines use ground sassafras leaves— known as filé powder—as a thickener. Likewise, both use what is known as the

"Holy Trinity" (equal parts green bell pepper, celery, and onion) in many of their dishes. But they head in separate directions from there. Creole cooking is in no way timid, but Cajun is "blow the top of your head off" hot! I think of it like this: Louisiana wearing a tuxedo while sitting at a white-linen-covered table—well that's Creole. But Louisiana wearing overalls, sipping a can of beer next to a smoky pecan fire, with a sweating forehead and a burning-hot tongue—now that's Cajun!

French Guiana; however, there is no history of it growing anywhere in the area. The Tabasco chile is very hot (7–8). It is bright red when ripe and measures approximately 1½-inches long and ⅜-inch wide. Its main use is in bottled hot sauce, and it also works quite well in salsas. Serrano chiles are a good substitute if a recipe calls for fresh Tabasco chiles. The name *Tabasco chile* comes from the city of Tabasco, Mexico, which in the 1850s was involved in brisk trading with New Orleans. The first

The cayenne chile is among the hottest.

The dominant chiles in this region are cayenne and Tabasco. The cayenne chile is among the hottest (8–9). Bright red when ripe and measuring up to 10 inches long by 1 inch wide, its main uses are in hot sauce or dried and ground into a powder. Well-known for its use in both Cajun and Creole cooking, it's also great in Asian dishes or fresh salsas. The name supposedly comes from the city of Cayenne in

seeds were imported by a banker named Maunsell White. In the 1860s White gave some of the pods to a friend by the name of Edmund McIlhenny. Although White had tried his hand making and selling a hot pepper sauce, it was McIlhenny who went back home to Avery Island (about 140 miles west of New Orleans) and changed the culinary world forever. He cultivated the chiles and tried several recipes until

he came up with the recipe for the world's first commercial hot sauce: Tabasco. For the first batch he used old cologne bottles that he rinsed out. This was done for two reasons. First, new bottles cost money, and more importantly, the cologne bottles had a shaker top on them. This caused his concentrated hot sauce to sprinkle rather than pour. He even made the labels by

is then fermented in white oak barrels for up to three years. When the fully aged mash is ready to process, a member of the McIlhenny family personally inspects it. Once approved the fully aged mash is blended with all-natural, high-grain vinegar. This is stirred on and off for about four weeks and then the seeds and chile skins are removed. The finished product is bot-

Tabasco is now producing some hot new sauce varieties.

hand. The worldwide headquarters for Tabasco is still on Avery Island and is run by Edmund McIlhenny's descendants. The chiles are handpicked at the peak of ripeness. To insure this, the field hands carry a Tabasco-red dowel, or *baton rouge*. They check the color of the chiles against the red dowel before picking them. They are mashed the same day they are picked, and mixed with a salt that is mined on Avery Island. The "mash," as it is called,

tled and shipped all over the world (105 countries at last count). Tabasco is now producing some hot new sauce varieties, including green jalapeño and a habanero sauce. I was so impressed with the habanero sauce that I wrote Mrs. McIlhenny a letter. I told her thanks for another great Tabasco product and that they were doing what they've been doing all along, showing the rest of the world how to make hot sauce the right way!

CRAWFISH ETOUFFÉE

Ask a Frenchman what etouffée *means and he will say "to choke"; ask a Cajun and he'll say "to smother."*
And that's exactly what this wonderful Cajun dish is—crawfish smothered in an amazing, complex,
spicy flavored sauce. I can only say one thing more about Crawfish Etouffée: make some . . . tonight.

⅓ cup canola or corn oil

¾ cup all-purpose flour

½ cup finely chopped green bell pepper

½ cup finely chopped brown onion

2 stalks celery, chopped fine

3 cups lobster, crawfish, or seafood stock

1 cup green onions, chopped very fine

3 pounds peeled crawfish tails

1 stick unsalted butter

4 cups Basic Cajun Rice (page 37)

Etouffée Spice Mix:

2 teaspoons cayenne pepper

2 teaspoons salt

1 teaspoon dried basil

1 teaspoon black pepper

1 teaspoon white pepper

½ teaspoon dried thyme

Mix all spices together and set aside.

In a large heavy iron skillet, heat the oil to medium high. With a long-handled whisk, carefully mix in the flour a little at a time until smooth. Keep whisking constantly for 3 to 5 minutes or until roux is dark red-brown. Do not let burn. Remove from heat. Immediately stir in bell pepper, onion, celery, and about half of Etouffée Spice Mix. Continue to stir until skillet cools down, about 4 to 5 minutes. Remove roux mixture from the skillet and set aside in the refrigerator to cool.

Once the roux is cool, bring 2 cups of the stock to a boil in a medium saucepan. Add the roux mixture and whisk constantly until roux is totally dissolved. Do not let burn. Remove from heat and set aside.

In a large saucepan over medium heat, sauté the green onions and crawfish in the butter for about 1 minute. Add remaining stock and roux mixture. Shake pan back and forth to mix flavors until butter is totally melted; stir gently if needed. Add remaining Etouffée Spice Mix, stirring well. Serve 3/4 cup Crawfish Etouffée over 1/2 cup Basic Cajun Rice.

Note: If sauce separates a little, add 1 or 2 tablespoons water or stock and shake pan until it binds.

Serves 8

Next to salt, chiles are the world's most popular seasonings.

CRAWFISH, CRAB, OR SHRIMP BOIL

This easy spice mix totally enhances the flavor of shellfish. When boiling crabs and crawfish, chefs often toss in some small red potatoes and corn, making a Cajun feast.

Spice Mixture:

½ cup sea salt

¼ cup pickling spices

3 tablespoons black peppercorns

2 tablespoons crushed red pepper flakes

2 tablespoons mustard seeds

1 tablespoon minced dried chives

1 tablespoon celery seeds

2 teaspoons dried Greek or Mediterranean oregano

2 teaspoons ground ginger

4 bay leaves, crushed

Mix all spice ingredients together well.

Place half of the Spice Mixture in 3 quarts of water and bring to a boil. Following instructions below, add seafood (use one of the three options below) and bring back to a boil. Remove pot from heat and allow to rest for 5 minutes.

Option 1: Follow recipe above, but add 4 pounds crawfish and 1 quartered lemon and boil for 15 minutes.

Option 2: Follow recipe above, but add 20 medium crabs and boil for 20 minutes. Try substituting white wine for a third of the cooking water.

Option 3: Follow recipe above, but add 4 pounds shrimp and allow to boil for 2 minutes. Try substituting beer for half of the cooking water.

Spice Mixture makes 2 batches
Serves 15 to 20

Roux

Years ago I was out having a breakfast of biscuits and gravy with my Grandma Rose. The gravy was thick like paste and had no flavor. I asked my grandma what was wrong with it. She said, "Some folks just don't know that they need to fry the flour." Although Grandma didn't use the term *roux,* she taught me a cooking lesson that has served me well over the years.

Using the proper roux will make all the difference not only in Cajun and Creole cooking but also in sauces and gravies in general. A roux is a 50-50 combination of flour and oil. The flour is added to hot oil about 1/3 at a time and fried, whisking constantly, to the desired color. The rule of thumb when using a roux is "hot stock cold roux, cold stock hot roux." If both are hot or cold, the roux will clump up rather than thicken.

In general the lighter the meat the darker the roux. Light fish and chicken breast uses dark reddish brown to sometimes almost black roux. Dark meat chicken and pork use a medium tan roux. Beef, duck, and wild game use light beige roux (some chefs use the exact opposite rule, light meat light roux). Before trying a black roux, try a dark reddish brown. The difference between a black roux and a burnt roux is about 3 seconds. With all rouxs, remove from heat just before the desired color. In the Cajun kitchen the cook stirs in the "Holy Trinity" (onion, celery, and green bell pepper) to stop the cooking and browning process. If you see little black specks in the roux, discard it and start over because it will have a burnt flavor.

CAJUN FIRECRACKER SHRIMP

I've seen this recipe under the name Cajun Barbecue Shrimp, Mardi Gras Shrimp and so on. I like this name because it's an explosion of flavor. A good bottle of cold Gewürztraminer and these shrimp are the start of a perfect romantic dinner for hot-and-spicy-food lovers.

1 pound (U–8*) large shrimp

1 teaspoon cayenne pepper

1 teaspoon granulated garlic

1 teaspoon freshly ground black pepper

½ teaspoon table salt

½ teaspoon dried whole thyme

½ teaspoon dried whole rosemary, crushed

⅛ teaspoon dried Greek oregano

4 tablespoons sweet butter

1 teaspoon Worcestershire sauce

1 cup dark beer, room temperature

¼ cup canned diced tomatoes, drained

Fresh rosemary

Squeeze of lemon

1 loaf French bread, warm

Clean the shrimp and rinse under cold water. Mix the spices together.

In a large sauté pan melt half of the butter. Add the spices, Worcestershire sauce, and then the shrimp. As soon as the shrimp start to change color, add the beer and stir well. Sauté until the sauce reduces by about half. Remove pan from heat. Remove shrimp from sauce to a serving dish. Swirl remaining butter and the tomatoes into sauce. Stir gently until sauce binds; then pour sauce over shrimp. Garnish with rosemary and a squeeze of lemon. Serve with fresh warm French bread to dip into the sauce.

Serves 4

*The U refers to the number of shrimp per pound. U–8 means 8 or less per pound. U–26 means 26 or less per pound. The lower the U number, the larger the shrimp.

Milk/Shellfish

Did you ever notice that sometimes shrimp or even lobster is a little dry and chewy? In the pages of this book you will find shellfish being marinated in milk. This is an old trick that I learned from my friend Bruce. He uses milk to make calamari tender. The enzymes in the milk break down the tissue fibers, making the shellfish tender, and the butterfat stays in the fibers, making it juicy.

CAJUN SOFT-SHELL CRABS ON BUNS

Every spring the crabs down in the delta molt, leaving their old shells behind. Whenever people try these delicious crabs for the first time they are a little wary. But one bite and they become lifelong disciples.

4 medium soft-shell crabs (ask your fish-
    monger to clean them)
2 cups milk
½ cup all-purpose flour
1 teaspoon granulated garlic
1 teaspoon Hungarian paprika
¾ teaspoon cayenne pepper
Oil for frying (for shellfish I like safflower)
4 (4-inch) freshly baked sandwich buns
Cajun Mayonnaise (see below)
Shredded iceberg lettuce

Soak the crabs in milk for 20 to 30 minutes. On a large flat plate, mix together the flour, garlic, paprika, and cayenne pepper. Deep-fry the crabs until crispy and deep golden brown. While crabs are frying, toast sandwich buns. Remove crabs from pan, place on a paper towel to drain, and salt immediately. Place one crab in each bun and top with Cajun Mayonnaise and lettuce.

Serves 4

CAJUN MAYONNAISE

Even the mayonnaise in Acadia has spices in it. You may think this is going overboard, but just wait until you try this with Cajun Soft-Shell Crabs on Buns (see above). You'll be using this stuff on everything!

1 cup mayonnaise
½ teaspoon Greek or Mediterranean
    oregano
½ teaspoon granulated garlic

½ teaspoon ground cumin
⅛ teaspoon cayenne pepper
⅛ teaspoon fresh ground black pepper

Combine all ingredients in a small nonreactive bowl. Cover and refrigerate overnight to blend flavors.

Makes 1 cup

Chile peppers were once used as currency!

BLACKENED REDFISH

Corporate America has embraced "blackening." I've seen everything blackened, from prime rib to sliced deli turkey. And I must say, in all cases it pales next to the authentic dish. It is the main reason that Cajun cooking exploded onto the American culinary scene in the early 1980s. Many people think that this is an age-old Cajun cooking technique. It was actually developed about twenty-five years ago by the famous Cajun-American cooking icon Paul Prudhomme for K-Paul's. It is delicious with any firm fish, but if you want to taste the original, use redfish!

2 redfish fillets

4 tablespoons unsalted butter, melted

Spice Mix:

1 tablespoon paprika

2 teaspoons salt

1 teaspoon cayenne pepper

1 teaspoon granulated garlic

1 teaspoon granulated onion

1 teaspoon freshly ground black pepper

½ teaspoon Greek or Mediterranean oregano

½ teaspoon dried thyme leaves

½ teaspoon white pepper

Lemon wedges

Sweet butter, melted

Use an outdoor burner to cook the fish. It's very smoky and a bit of a fire hazard, so be careful and keep the kids away. Heat a large cast-iron skillet or griddle over high heat until well beyond the smoking stage, at least 5 minutes.

Quickly rinse the redfish under cold water and dry with a paper towel. Coat both sides of the redfish with melted butter. Mix the spices together and sprinkle over both sides of the fish, patting it into place. Place both fillets in the hot iron skillet and top with 1 teaspoon melted butter. Watch out for a flare-up. Fry until the bottom side of the fish is crisp and just lightly charred, about 2 to 3 minutes, depending on the thickness. Carefully flip the redfish and top the other side with 1 teaspoon melted butter, fry about 2 minutes, or until done. Serve immediately on a warm dinner plate with a slice of lemon and melted butter on the side.

Serves 2

Oregano

In this chapter I suggest using Greek or Mediterranean oregano, which has a much sweeter flavor that its Mexican counterpart. As we move west we will switch to Mexican oregano, which has a flatter flavor that is essential in Southwest and Mexican cooking.

FILÉ GUMBO WITH CAJUN FRIED CHICKEN AND ANDOUILLE SAUSAGE

The Cajun fried chicken in this recipe is out of this world all by itself. Combine it with Andouille sausage, let it stew in this wonderful gumbo, and you've got a red-hot dish that will be a family favorite.

1 chicken, cut into 4 pieces

2 cups buttermilk

Dredge:

¾ cup all-purpose flour

1 tablespoon salt

1 tablespoon paprika

1 tablespoon brown sugar

2 teaspoons cayenne pepper

1 teaspoon white pepper

1 teaspoon thyme

1 teaspoon granulated garlic

Oil for frying

½ pound Andouille sausage

4 tablespoons sweet butter

1½ cups minced white onion

1½ cups minced green bell pepper

1½ cups minced celery

1 tablespoon Louisiana hot sauce

2 tablespoons filé powder

½ teaspoon white pepper

½ teaspoon Greek oregano

½ teaspoon cayenne pepper

½ teaspoon kosher salt

½ teaspoon granulated garlic

6 cups chicken broth

1 cup tomato sauce

1 cup tomatoes, peeled and seeded

1 pound okra, sliced into ½-inch rings

Soak the chicken pieces in cold buttermilk for 45 minutes.

Meanwhile, mix the dredge together; then heat 1 inch of oil in a large Dutch oven. Remove the chicken from the buttermilk and dredge in flour mixture. Tap off excess flour. Fry each side of the chicken until browned, about 6 minutes. Set aside. (If you're just making fried chicken and not the Gumbo, fry chicken for 12 minutes per side.)

Pour most of the excess oil out of pan, leaving a few tablespoons, and brown the sausage. Set aside.

Melt the butter in the Dutch oven. Add onion, bell pepper, celery, hot sauce, filé powder, white pepper, oregano, cayenne, salt, and granulated garlic. Sauté until soft but not browned, stirring constantly. Deglaze the pan with the chicken broth and then add the tomato sauce, tomatoes, and okra. Bring to a boil, reduce heat, slice the sausage, and add along with the chicken; simmer for at least 1 hour. Serve with Basic Cajun Rice (page 37).

Serves 6 regular people or 2 Cajuns

SLOW-ROASTED PORK WITH CAJUN BARBECUE SAUCE AU JUSTIN

I like this best slow-smoked using pecan. Start the fire early and keep an eye on it all day. The backyard comes alive with the heavenly aroma while you sip cold beer and wait for the feast.

1 (4-pound) pork shoulder

Cajun Rub:

1 tablespoon paprika

1 tablespoon kosher salt

1 tablespoon brown sugar

2 teaspoons white pepper

1 teaspoon black pepper

1 teaspoon cayenne pepper

½ teaspoon ground thyme

Mix the dry ingredients together and rub well into the exterior of the pork roast. Wrap in plastic and allow it to rest overnight in the refrigerator. If you are in a hurry, you can let it rest for half an hour, but overnight is much better!

The rule when roasting pork is "low and slow," so pop it in the oven, grill, or smoker at somewhere around 250 degrees and roast it until it reaches an internal temperature of 165 degrees. Remove from heat and allow it to rest for 20 minutes before slicing. Serve with Cajun Barbecue Sauce au Justin (see below) on the side.

Serves 8 to 12

CAJUN BARBECUE SAUCE AU JUSTIN

This is a modern adaptation of the famous Cajun cook Justin Wilson's barbecue sauce. Unlike other barbecue sauces, it's made to be served on the side as a finishing sauce, not for basting while slow cooking. As Justin said, it's "garontee to warm the belly!"

2 cups finely chopped brown onion

½ green bell pepper, chopped fine

¼ cup extra virgin olive oil

4 cloves garlic, minced

2 cups ketchup

1 cup A-1 Steak Sauce

½ cup dry red wine

¼ cup Louisiana hot sauce (Trappy's or Red Devil)

¼ cup red wine vinegar

2 tablespoons brown sugar

2 tablespoons freshly squeezed lemon juice

1 tablespoon very finely chopped fresh flat-leaf parsley

1 tablespoon salt

1 teaspoon celery seed

½ teaspoon cayenne pepper

½ teaspoon white pepper

In a saucepan sauté onions and bell pepper in the olive oil until translucent. Add garlic and soften. Add all other ingredients. Bring to a low boil and stir well. Cover, reduce heat to low, and barely simmer for 2 to 3 hours. Serve with roasted meats or poultry.

Makes about 6 cups

RED BEANS AND RICE

This is one of my favorite examples of Cajun comfort food. On a cold winter day I love to make up a big batch. This is also a good place for novice cooks to start to develop their own flavors. Try substituting your favorite sausage for the salt pork or adding different vegetables. This recipe is more a suggestion than an exact formula. Any Cajun cook that is worth his salt will throw in whatever is hanging out in the fridge!

1 pound red kidney beans

1 tablespoon white vinegar

1 pound salt pork

1 green bell pepper, chopped fine

1 brown onion, chopped fine

1 celery stalk, chopped fine

2 cloves garlic, minced

Dash of Tabasco Sauce

1 teaspoon Italian seasoning

2 jalapeño peppers, whole and pierced

Sort through beans removing any foreign material. Soak the beans overnight in water with vinegar. In the morning, discard water, rinse beans well, and set aside.

Boil the salt pork in water for 5 minutes; discard the water. This takes some of the salt out of the pork. Place the pork in a big pot with fresh hot water. Add the beans, bell pepper, onion, celery, garlic, Tabasco, Italian seasoning, and jalapeños. Simmer for 2 to 3 hours until gravy is thick and beans are tender. Prior to serving, add a pinch of Italian seasoning, salt, and black pepper to taste. Serve with Basic Cajun Rice (page 37).

Serves 6 to 8

Thanksgiving or Christmas!

BOURBON SWEET POTATOES

This is one of the most decadent side dishes I've ever had. Heavy cream, butter, bourbon, and brown sugar—next to any roasted poultry, it's simply heaven. (Do these pants make me look fat?)

3 sweet potatoes, peeled and cut into
   1-inch cubes

½ cup chopped pecans

1 teaspoon butter

3 tablespoons soft butter

4 tablespoons firmly packed brown sugar

4 tablespoons heavy cream

3 tablespoons bourbon

¼ teaspoon cinnamon

Pinch of nutmeg

Salt to taste

Boil the sweet potatoes 30 minutes or until tender. Meanwhile, sauté the pecans in 1 teaspoon of butter for 2 minutes. Drain the sweet potatoes and place in a food processor while still warm. Add 3 tablespoons soft butter, brown sugar, cream, bourbon, cinnamon, nutmeg, and salt. Puree, adding more cream as needed to make the potatoes soft and creamy. Top with sautéed pecans.

Serves 6

According to the McIlhenny Company, the U.S. Territory of Guam is the world's largest per capita consumer of Tabasco Sauce.

BRABANT POTATOES

These delicious, spicy little devils are a great example of Cajun cooking. They're not just hot—they have layers of spice flavors. Don't let this scare you away, but I call it the "barn-door effect" because the flavors are about as subtle as getting hit in the face with a barn door!

2 pounds white potatoes, unpeeled
2½ quarts water
1½ tablespoons table salt
Canola oil for frying

Spice Mixture:

1½ teaspoons table salt
¼ teaspoon granulated garlic
¼ teaspoon onion powder
¼ teaspoon white pepper
¼ teaspoon freshly ground black pepper
⅛ teaspoon paprika
⅛ teaspoon cayenne pepper
⅛ teaspoon ground cumin

Wash the unpeeled potatoes and cut into 1-inch cubes. Combine water with salt and bring to a rapid boil. Add the potatoes to the boiling water, cover, and cook for 6 to 7 minutes until just barely fork tender. Remove potatoes from boiling water, rinse well under cold water, and place in a medium-size mixing bowl.

In a large skillet, pour canola oil 1 inch deep and heat to 350 degrees. While the oil heats, combine all spice mixture ingredients in a small bowl. Sprinkle potatoes with spice mixture, carefully tossing until they are evenly coated. Take care not to break up the potato cubes while tossing. Fry the potatoes in batches, small enough to make only one layer in the skillet at a time, until golden brown. Remove from skillet and drain on a paper towel. Serve immediately.

Serves 6

BASIC CAJUN RICE

Every now and then I'll go out for Cajun food and the cook will do a fantastic job, but the dish will be served with plain old white rice. If the rice isn't real, then the meal isn't real (and that's the real deal!).

1 cup converted rice

1¼ cups pork stock or chicken broth

3 teaspoons sweet butter, melted

½ celery stalk, chopped fine

1 tablespoon finely chopped bell pepper

1 tablespoon finely chopped brown onion

¼ teaspoon salt

⅛ teaspoon cayenne pepper

⅛ teaspoon onion powder

⅛ teaspoon granulated garlic

⅛ teaspoon white pepper

⅛ teaspoon black pepper

Combine all ingredients in a small baking dish. Mix well and cover with a lid or tightly with foil. Bake at 350 degrees for about 1 hour and 10 minutes, or until rice is tender. Serve immediately.

Serves 4 to 5

One noted scientific journal reports that drinking a quart and a half of Louisiana-style hot sauce will cause death by respiratory failure if your body weight is 140 pounds or less.

DIRTY RICE

The original recipe for Dirty Rice calls for the addition of chicken gizzards and chicken fat. I've omitted those ingredients because this dish is fantastic without them. But, hey, it's your rice, so do what you want.

2 brown onions, chopped fine

4 celery stalks, chopped fine

1 green bell pepper, chopped fine

2 cloves garlic, minced

2 tablespoons light olive oil

1½ pounds ground pork

2 teaspoons Louisiana hot sauce
   (Trappy's or Red Devil)

3 teaspoons cayenne pepper

1½ tablespoons Hungarian paprika

1½ teaspoons dry mustard

1 teaspoon ground cumin

1 teaspoon salt

1 teaspoon freshly ground black pepper

1 teaspoon Mediterranean or Greek oregano

1 teaspoon ground dried thyme

3 tablespoons sweet butter

4 cups pork stock or chicken broth

1 pound chicken livers, chopped

2 cups long-grain rice

1 bay leaf

Using a large heavy skillet with lid over medium-high heat, sauté the onions, celery, bell pepper, and garlic in 1 tablespoon of the oil until soft but not browned; remove mixture from pan and set aside. Add the pork and the other tablespoon of oil to the pan and fry until well browned. Add the sautéed onion mixture. Then add the hot sauce and spices. Stir thoroughly, scraping bottom of the pan well. Add the butter and stir in until fully melted. Reduce heat to medium and cook about 8 minutes, stirring constantly and scraping bottom of the pan as you go. Add the stock and deglaze the pan by stirring well until any mixture sticking to the pan bottom comes loose. Add the chicken livers, rice, and bay leaf, and bring to a boil. Cover pan, reduce heat to low, and cook for 20 minutes without lifting the lid. Remove bay leaf, stir well, and serve immediately.

Serves 8 to 10

CAJUN FRIED ZUCCHINI

This is real Cajun—hot, spicy, and delicious. This recipe also works well with eggplant. You will occasionally see this dish served lightly sprinkled with powered sugar!

Spice Mix:

1 teaspoon salt

½ teaspoon white pepper

½ teaspoon cayenne pepper

½ teaspoon freshly ground black pepper

½ teaspoon Hungarian paprika

½ teaspoon granulated onion

½ teaspoon granulated garlic

¼ teaspoon dried thyme

⅛ teaspoon dried basil

2 cups zucchini, peeled and chopped

1 cup all-purpose flour

1 cup plain breadcrumbs

1 cup milk

2 eggs

Canola oil for frying

Mix the spices together and sprinkle zucchini with 1 or 2 teaspoons of the mix. Place the flour and breadcrumbs in separate bowls. Add 1 teaspoon of the spice mix to the flour and 1 teaspoon to the bread-crumbs and blend well. In a third bowl combine the milk and egg and beat well with a fork.

Pour 1 inch of oil in a skillet and heat to 350 degrees. Just before fry-ing, dredge the zucchini in the flour and shake off excess. Using a slotted spoon, quickly coat zucchini with the milk mixture and then with the breadcrumbs, shaking off excess. Fry the zucchini in hot oil until dark golden brown, about 2 to 3 minutes, making sure to separate the pieces as you drop them into the hot oil. Drain, lightly salt, and serve immediately.

Serves 4

CREOLE OKRA AND TOMATOES

This is an excellent example of the difference between Creole and Cajun cooking. The use of tomatoes and butter is very Creole and this dish, depending on how much pepper you use, can be very mild. Either way, you'll love it.

4 tablespoons sweet butter

1 large brown onion, chopped fine

1 stalk celery, chopped fine

¼ green bell pepper, chopped fine

4 cups fresh sliced okra, rinsed very well

6 plum tomatoes, coarsely chopped

Salt and freshly ground black pepper to taste

In large skillet, sauté the onion and celery in the butter, until soft. Add the bell pepper, okra, and tomatoes. Reduce heat, cover, and simmer 20 minutes, stirring occasionally. Season to taste.

Serves 8 to 10

Granulated or Powdered?

In reading these recipes, you may notice I suggest granulated garlic and onion, which come from the heart of these bulbs; the powders use the exterior skins. The granulated forms have a greater concentration of oil and thus more flavor.

BEIGNETS WITH CREOLE BUTTERSCOTCH SAUCE

It seems many cultures have a version of sweet fried bread for dessert. There are sopapillas, buñeulos, and good ol', all-American doughnuts to name a few. Beignets are more delicate and subtle in flavor. It's that elegant Creole feel in a simple dessert.

Vegetable oil or shortening for deep-frying

Dough:

1 cup water

1 stick sweet butter

¼ teaspoon salt

1 teaspoon granulated sugar

1 cup plus 2 tablespoons all-purpose flour, sifted

4 large eggs

1 teaspoon vanilla extract

Confectioners' sugar

In a Dutch oven or deep-sided pan, preheat 3 inches of oil to 375 degrees. Meanwhile, bring the water, butter, salt, and granulated sugar to a rapid boil in a small saucepan. Remove from heat and add the flour, stirring vigorously. Cook the mixture over low heat while beating constantly, until the ingredients are thoroughly mixed and the dough cleanly leaves the sides of the pan and forms a ball.

Remove the pan from the heat; add the eggs one at a time, beating well after each. Beat the dough either by hand or with an electric mixer set at medium speed until it is smooth and shiny; then stir in the vanilla.

Once the oil reaches the correct temperature, carefully drop the dough by teaspoonfuls into the hot oil. Fry the beignets in batches, turning them a few times, for about 3 minutes or until golden brown. Carefully remove with a slotted spoon and place on paper towels to drain. Sprinkle beignets with confectioners' sugar or Creole Butterscotch Sauce (see next page). Serve warm!

Serves 6 to 8

CREOLE BUTTERSCOTCH SAUCE

This easy sauce is a must with warm beignets (see previous page). But also try it with your favorite dessert.

¾ cup light brown sugar

⅓ cup light corn syrup

1 tablespoon sweet butter

½ cup heavy cream

½ teaspoon pure vanilla extract

Bring the brown sugar, corn syrup, and butter to a boil in a medium saucepan, stirring constantly. Remove from heat and stir in cream and vanilla. Serve warm.

Makes about 1½ cups

Famous chili cook and author Audy Householder suggests drinking cayenne pepper tea to fight off a cold!

CAJUN BOURBON BREAD PUDDING

I love this simple, elegant dessert. My mom made bread pudding when I was a kid and it reminds me of being in her kitchen!

1 large loaf French bread, sliced ½-inch
   thick and air-dried overnight

8 large eggs

¼ cup flour

1½ cups pure maple syrup

2 pints half-and-half

1 teaspoon pure vanilla extract

½ teaspoon ground cinnamon

¼ teaspoon ground nutmeg

¼ teaspoon salt

½ cup chopped assorted dried fruit

½ cup toasted pecans

Preheat the oven to 375 degrees. Butter a medium baking dish. In a food processor lightly beat the eggs. Add flour and beat until smooth. Add maple syrup, half-and-half, vanilla, cinnamon, nutmeg, and salt. Beat until well mixed. Layer the bread in the baking dish, overlapping like the scales on a fish, into three or four rows. Ladle the egg mixture over the bread slices and allow the mixture to soak into the bread for 5 to 8 minutes. Sprinkle the dried fruit over the bread. Chop up half of the pecans, and sprinkle all the pecans over the bread.

Place a sheet pan in the middle rack of the oven and fill with water. Place a baking rack on top of four ramekins or spacers (bricks will do in a pinch) in the pan of water. Cover the top of the bread pudding with foil and place on the rack. Bake for 1/2 hour, rotate the dish to ensure even baking, and bake for 1/2 hour more. Remove foil and bake until pudding is set and golden brown, about 15 minutes. Drizzle with Cajun Bourbon Sauce (see next page) and serve.

Serves 8 or more

CAJUN BOURBON SAUCE

Delicious on any warm baked dessert!

½ cup sugar

½ cup water

2 tablespoons sweet butter

2 or 3 tablespoons bourbon

Bring water and sugar to a simmer until sugar dissolves. Remove from heat and swirl in butter and bourbon.

Serves 4 to 6

The jalapeño was the first pepper to be taken into outer space—it was aboard an early manned space flight.

CATTLEMEN

AS WE CROSS THE LOUISIANA STATE LINE INTO TEXAS, we find a
group of people who, although gentle, friendly, and extremely
polite, are as tough and unyielding as the land conquered by
the ranchers, cowboys, and vaqueros who came before
them. A wealthy New York financier once said of this seemingly endless prairie of twisters, cactus, and rattlesnakes, "If
I owned both Texas and Hell, I'd live in Hell and rent Texas
out!" The book *Cowboy Cocktails* by Grady Spears and Brigit
Binns defines a Texas cowboy as someone who "could
'rassle' a thousand-pound bull to the ground, brand him
with a hot iron, and then eat his cojones for breakfast."

Texas is a nation unto itself. When traveling abroad, average U.S. citizens introduce themselves as Americans. But not those from Texas . . . no, they're Texans. The big ranches and the cattlemen who ran them are the embodiment of the American West. Since a large portion of Texas was once part of Mexico, native Texans practically have a mixture of tequila and jalapeño juice running through their veins! It's the

the cattle drives in the mid-1800s, while heading north from Texas, the chuck-wagon cooks found chiles growing wild. Vegetables and kitchen staples were always in short supply, so they used these chiles along with salt, black pepper, and whatever spices they might be able to muster up to create a hearty, spicy, flavorful sort of beef stew. It was so popular that the cooks would save the seeds from the chiles and

Whatever the origin, Texas red chili is here to stay.

birthplace of buckaroos, Texas swing, Willie Nelson, Tex-Mex, Lone Star Beer, the margarita, and, more importantly, red chili and the all-American barbecue! Since I'm a barbecue and chili cook from Arizona, and damn proud of it, this fact gripes me to no end!

My grandfather used to say, "It's a damn poor story that a Texan can't improve upon!" So when in Texas, sorting out the true facts may be a chore. Take the origins of Texas red chili. One story has it that on

toss them under thorny trees and around cactuses where the animals might leave them alone. This would ensure a good chile crop for next year's trail drive.

Another story told by chili historian Floyd Cogan, and the version I like best, goes something like this: In the Texas prisons around 1850 dubious purchasing agents would buy poor to sometimes-rancid meat and pocket the savings. The cooks inside (most likely fearing retribution) would try to hide the bad taste by chopping and mixing it with lots of chiles and spices, and then adding water, creating a red chili gruel. It is said that by 1890 jailhouse chili was so popular that the inmates would rate how hard the time was in a particular institution based on the chili it served. And in extreme cases (remember what my grandpa said), they would break parole and get locked up again just for the chili.

There are several different variations of these stories. One told by noted chili scholar E. De Grolyer tells of pounding chiles, salt, beef, and fat together. This would later be added to water and boiled, creating red chili. The concoction was known as the "Pemmican of the Southwest." I personally believe the origin of Texas red chili was a combination of all three stories, with a fair amount of help from the Mexicans living throughout what is now called Texas. Chili is a regional descendant of the many chile-based dishes dating back to the Aztec, Incan, and Mayan cultures.

Whatever the origin, Texas red chili is here to stay. In the early 1890s, Dewitt Pendery and William Gebhardt both started producing ground chili powders. Pendery advertised, "The health giving properties of hot chile peppers have no equal. They give tone to the alimentary canal, regulating the functions, giving a natural appetite, and promoting healthy action of the kidneys, skin, and lymphatics." Like all things surrounding chili, there is an ongoing debate concerning who was the first to produce a commercial chili powder, but there's no argument that it was a Texan. Both Pendery's and Gebhardt's very successful companies ship red chili powder from Texas throughout the world to this day.

In 1893 the Chicago World's Fair had a popular attraction called the San Antonio Chili Stand. It offered "A Bowl O' Red" and was reminiscent of the famous San Antonio street vendors known as Chili Queens. The Chili Queens had been in business on the streets of San Antonio for about fifty years when they were shut down in 1937 for public health reasons. There was such a public outcry that the city's mayor, Maury Maverick, allowed the stands to reopen in 1939, but a few years later World War II broke out and they were closed for good.

Although many chili historians believe the first chili cook-off was held in Terlingua, Texas, in 1967, newspaper articles from *The Daily Times Herald* of Dallas prove this to be false. On October 5, 1952, at the Texas State Fair, Mrs. F. G. Ventura of Dallas, Texas, became the first "World Champion Chili Cook," a title that she held for the next fifteen years.

The Terlingua cook-off in 1967 is, by far, the best known. It all started when New York City writer and humorist H. Allen Smith wrote an article for the August 1967 issue of *Holiday* magazine. The article, entitled "Nobody Knows More About Chili Than I Do," stated that no Texan could make proper chili. Smith further went on to give his recipe, which included, of all things, beans. He had

gone too far. Frank X. Tolbert, Texan and author of the famous book *A Bowl Of Red,* attacked Smith in the press and the feud was on. Finally, the small mining town of Terlingua—in the middle of nowhere—was selected to settle the argument. More than 5,000 people from all over the U.S. showed up to witness a cook-off between Texas chili champ Wick Fowler and H. Allen Smith. The contest was called a draw when the blindfolded, tie-breaking judge, Dave Witts, took a mouthful of the chili and promptly spat it out on the referee's foot. Gary Cartwright, a writer for *Sports Illustrated,* noted, "Then he went into convulsions. He rammed a white handkerchief down his throat as though he were cleaning a rifle barrel, and in an agonizing whisper pronounced himself unable to go on."

Then, in 1977 the Texas State Legislature proclaimed chili con carne the Official Texas State Dish.

There are several colorful descriptions of red chili; my favorite comes from Spanish priests preaching against the consumption of

chili, saying it was "as hot as Hell's brimstone" and "the Devil's soup." Texas may be proud of chili but Mexicans . . . well that's a different story. A Mexican dictionary from the mid-1900s defines chili as "a detestable dish, sold from Texas to New York City and erroneously described as Mexican." Likewise, Mexicans will tell you that the Mexican food other development was the advent of the combination dinner, the infamous #3 plate that offers a taco, a cheese enchilada, and a tostada, with rice, refried beans, chips, and salsa. Tex-Mex became so popular north of the border that for many of us who grew up in the '50s, '60s, and '70s, it was our first taste of Mexican food.

The king of all chiles is, without a doubt, the jalapeño.

in Texas is not Mexican food at all, but instead is something called Tex-Mex.

Tex-Mex cooking, like so many foods that have developed throughout the Chile Belt, is a blending of cultures. It finds its roots in the Norteno style of cooking. Many of the dishes can be found in northern Mexico. However the Tex-Mex versions have been changed and adapted over time, using more readily available ingredients. For example, Monterey Jack cheese is substituted for the Queso Ranchero used in Mexico, or ground beef for the original shredded beef used in Mexican tacos. The

The all-American barbecue grill also has been attributed to cattle ranching in the Lone Star State. As the story goes, at a roundup, the cook would dig a long pit and fill it with mesquite. The cowboys would heat up their branding irons in the fire. After the coals had died down a bit, the cook would lay the branding irons across the pit, creating a crude grill. Large chunks of beef would then be slow-cooked. This method was unpredictable at best, but the idea helped develop the barbecues used in backyards all over the world today.

Although many chiles are used in this region (and the list keeps getting longer as new ideas are incorporated into the local cuisine), a few chiles have been used for a century or more and really stand out.

The king of all chiles is, without a doubt, the jalapeño. It derives its name from the city of Xalapa in Veracruz, Mexico. Although not grown there today, it reportedly thrived there centuries ago. Bright green, bullet shaped, and measuring approximately 2 1/2 inches in length, it has a medium-hot heat level (5–7). Texas is by far the largest producer and consumer of jalapeños in the U.S. They are used fresh (for salsa and Tex-Mex dishes), pickled (for nachos), and smoked (known as *chipotle* or *moro*).

Although not as well known in the U.S., the poblano is my favorite chile. Named for the Puebla region of Mexico, it's a dark green to almost black chile with a rich, earthy flavor. Due to crossbreeding, it can run from very mild (2–3) to medium hot (6–7). A quick—though sometimes inaccurate—method for telling the heat level of a green chile is "the darker the skin the hotter the chile." When mature, the chile is about 2 1/2 to 3 inches wide and 4 to 5 inches long, tapering from top to bottom in a heart shape. The very best poblanos are grown in central Mexico and are usually dried. Dried poblanos are known as *chile ancho* or *mulato,* and the premium dried poblanos seldom seen outside of Mexico are called *primero.* In Texas poblanos are mainly used for chile rellenos, but they also can be used in traditional green chile stew or roasted, peeled, and drizzled with lime and a sprinkle of Mexican oregano.

Whether you believe the Texas ranchers influenced the Mexican vaqueros or the other way around, the spicy foods developed here are unique and loved the world over. You may want to loosen your belt a notch or two because you're in for some down-home Texas-style cooking!

RED-HOT SOUTH TEXAS SHRIMP EN ESCABECHE

Although this is a great appetizer, I love it as a salad on butter lettuce with a few slices of avocado, warm French bread, and a good crisp sauvignon blanc!

1 lemon, sliced

1 cup celery tops

½ cup Crab Boil spice (ask your fish monger)

1½ tablespoons kosher salt

½ teaspoon black pepper

2½ pounds raw medium shrimp, peeled and deveined

2 medium white onions, sliced thin

12 bay leaves

1¾ cups canola oil

2 cups white vinegar

1½ tablespoons sea salt

1 tablespoon crushed red chile

2 teaspoons pink peppercorns

⅓ cup capers in brine

¼ cup celery seeds

15 cloves garlic, cut in half

2 sprigs fresh thyme

8 to 10 pickled bird peppers, or 2 pickled jalapeño chiles, cut in quarters lengthwise

5 dashes Tabasco Sauce

1 teaspoon white pepper

1 teaspoon black pepper

Fill a stockpot halfway and add the lemon, celery, Crab Boil, salt, and black pepper. Bring to a rolling boil and add the shrimp. Stir well and remove from heat. Allow shrimp to stew in the hot liquid for 10 minutes; then remove shrimp and plunge into an ice bath to stop cooking. Drain the shrimp well.

Layer the shrimp, onion slices, and bay leaves in a glass bowl. Emulsify the oil, vinegar, and salt with an electric hand whisk or in the blender. Then stir in remaining ingredients. Pour over layered shrimp. Cover and refrigerate for 24 to 48 hours, stirring every 6 to 8 hours.

Serves 8 as an appetizer

TEXAS-STYLE "CHICKEN SHACK" FRIED CHICKEN

Trust me, this is the real deal. I have an old friend from down South who tells me the secret to good fried chicken is cold chicken and hot grease.

Marinade:

1 quart buttermilk

1 tablespoon salt

1 tablespoon soy sauce

2 teaspoons Worcestershire sauce

1½ teaspoons white pepper

2 teaspoons granulated garlic

1 teaspoon sugar

1 teaspoon ancho chile powder

1 teaspoon cayenne pepper

Breasts, legs, thighs, and wings from two
frying chickens, with skin

Dredge:

3 cups all-purpose flour

1 tablespoon salt

1 teaspoon cayenne pepper

1 teaspoon white pepper

1 teaspoon granulated garlic

½ teaspoon ancho chile powder

Canola oil for frying

In a large nonreactive container, whisk all marinade ingredients together. Place the chicken in the marinade so that all the pieces are submerged. Cover and refrigerate overnight, stirring twice.

Stir together the dredge ingredients. Remove the chicken from the marinade, discard marinade, and drain the chicken for a few minutes. Dredge the chicken in the flour mixture and place on a cookie sheet so that the pieces are not touching. Place the cookie sheet in the refrigerator for 15 minutes.

Pour 2 inches of oil into a large iron frying pan and heat to 375 degrees. Take only as much chicken from the refrigerator as will fit in the frying pan in one layer and carefully place it in the oil a piece at a time. Fry one side for 12 minutes, turn and fry the other side for 12 minutes or until golden brown. Serve with mashed potatoes, gravy, green beans, and plenty of iced tea.

Serves 12

"It can only truly be Texas red if it walks the thin line just this side of indigestibility: Damning the mouth that eats it and defying the stomach to digest it, the ingredients are hardly willing to lie in the same pot together."   John Thorne, *Simple Cooking*

CHICKEN-FRIED STEAK ALA JACK YOUNG

My Uncle Jack was raised during the Great Depression in Whitewright, Texas, population around eighty. He taught me everything a person needs to know about playing poker and making the perfect chicken-fried steak. With chicken-fried steak the trick is to soak the pounded steak in buttermilk for exactly 20 minutes. Any longer and it will fall apart on you. As far as the poker goes, well . . . some secrets will have to stay in the family.

2 (1-pound) top-round steaks, ½-inch thick,
   cut in half, fat removed, yielding 4 steaks

2 cups buttermilk

Oil for frying

2 eggs

Pinch of salt

2 dashes Louisiana hot sauce

1 cup all-purpose flour

2 teaspoons salt

1 teaspoon white pepper

½ teaspoon cayenne pepper

½ teaspoon black pepper

3 tablespoons all-purpose flour

1½ cups cold milk

Salt and pepper to taste

Place the steaks between two pieces of plastic wrap (I use a plastic bag) and pound to 1/4-inch thick with a meat mallet. Place the steaks in a nonreactive bowl or baking dish of buttermilk and set a timer for 20 minutes.

Meanwhile, heat up a large iron skillet with 1/8-inch oil. Beat the eggs with the pinch of salt and the Louisiana hot sauce. Mix 1 cup flour with salt, white pepper, cayenne pepper, and black pepper.

When the timer goes off, remove the steaks from the buttermilk and pat dry. Dip in the egg wash and dredge in the flour mixture, and then repeat the process.

Depending on the size of your skillet, it may be necessary to fry the steaks in batches. It's better to have extra room around the steaks than for them to be crowded in the skillet. The pan should be hot but not smoking. Brown one side of the steaks and turn; this should take about 1 minute. Reduce heat to medium, cover pan, and cook for 7 minutes. Remove cover and fry for 2 minutes more. Turn and fry uncovered for 3 minutes more; steak should be nice and crispy. Remove from skillet and keep warm.

After all the steaks are fried, drain all but about 3 tablespoons of the oil from the skillet. Shake in the 3 tablespoons of flour and fry over medium heat until golden brown, whisking constantly. Continue whisking while adding the milk. Bring to a simmer while whisking until gravy becomes thick. Adjust seasoning and serve the steaks covered in the gravy.

Serves 4

SWEET-AND-SPICY PEPSI-COLA BABY BACK RIBS

Being a barbecue purest, I'm a guy who uses rubs and believes that barbecue sauce should be served on the side. However, it's not just about me, so if you want the stickiest, gooiest, twelve-napkin-usingest ribs you've ever eaten, try this recipe. And wear an old shirt—they're more than messy!

1 cup Pepsi-Cola

1 cup tomato sauce

½ cup dark brown sugar

½ cup dark molasses

½ cup white vinegar

1 (6-ounce) can tomato paste

2 tablespoons sweet butter

¼ cup Worcestershire sauce

2 tablespoons balsamic vinegar

2 tablespoons maple syrup

1 tablespoon dry mustard

1 tablespoon ancho chile powder or paprika

½ tablespoon kosher salt

½ tablespoon freshly ground black pepper

1 teaspoon cayenne pepper

1 teaspoon marjoram

1 teaspoon granulated garlic

1 teaspoon onion powder

2 dashes Tabasco Habanero Sauce

2 racks of baby back ribs

Mix all ingredients together and simmer over low heat until thick enough to coat the back of a metal spoon. Baste baby back ribs with this sauce while slow-smoking or barbecuing.

Serves 4

 Famous Big Band leader Harry James once said, "Next to music there is nothing that lifts the spirits and strengthens the soul more than a good bowl of chili," and "Congress should pass a law making it mandatory for all restaurants serving chili to follow a Texas recipe."

TEXAS RED CHILI

The following recipe is more of a starting place on the road to becoming a chili cook. My advice is to follow my recipe exactly the first time and then ask yourself a few questions: Was it hot enough, or salty enough? What about the level of garlic or cumin? From there, start adjusting and keep notes. There's nothing more frustrating than making the perfect chili and then thinking, "Now how did I make that?" Trust me, it will haunt you for the rest of your life.

½ white onion, chopped fine

3 cloves garlic, finely minced

1 tablespoon canola oil

1½ pounds ground beef

½ pound ground pork

¼ cup ancho chile powder, mild New Mexico
   chile powder, or paprika

2 teaspoons ground cumin

1 teaspoon Mexican oregano

½ teaspoon cayenne pepper

1 (28-ounce) can chicken broth

1 (8-ounce) can tomato sauce

1 bottle Lone Star Beer

Salt to taste

In a large frying pan, sauté the onion and garlic in the oil until soft but not browned. Add the meat and continue cooking until brown. Add the chili powder, cumin, oregano, and cayenne pepper and stir well. Then add the chicken broth, tomato sauce, and beer; stir well. Bring to a boil over medium-high heat for 15 minutes. Reduce heat to low and simmer for an hour, stirring often. Salt to taste. If it gets too thick, add a little more beer. Serve in big bowls with ice-cold Lone Star Beer, cheddar cheese, chopped white onion, and saltine crackers.

Serves 6

"Chili concocted outside of Texas is usually a weak, apologetic imitation of the real thing. One of the first things I do when I get home to Texas is to have a bowl of red. There is simply nothing better."
Lyndon B. Johnson, 36th President of the United States

AVOCADO SOUR CREAM

No, it's not guacamole—it's creamier, smoother, and a little more sophisticated. Try it with your favorite Tex-Mex dish or with hot corn chips, pico de gallo, and a frozen margarita.

2 ripe Hass avocados, seeded and peeled

1 cup sour cream

½ cup whipping cream

3 dashes Louisiana hot sauce

Salt and black pepper to taste

Mash the avocado well. Whisk in the sour cream and whipping cream. Whisk well and then stir in the other ingredients. Cover and refrigerate. Use within 6 hours.

Makes about 2½ cups

TEX-MEX TACOS

This recipe calls for premade taco shells. If you want, you can fry your own corn tortillas with the meat mixture inside. Make sure to drain them on a paper towel before filling them with the toppings. My friend, Western author Bob "Boze" Bell, fries his tacos while holding the tortilla closed with an old pair of pliers! I think the reason we never get poisoned from this practice has something to do with the amount of tequila we consume while cooking!

1 tablespoon vegetable oil

1 small white onion, chopped fine

3 cloves garlic

4 Roma tomatoes, diced

2 pounds ground beef

1 pound ground pork

1 large bunch cilantro, rinsed and chopped

Salt and pepper to taste

12 taco shells

Toppings:

shredded lettuce, finely chopped white
    onion, avocado slices, salsa, tomato, and
    cheddar cheese

In a skillet, sauté the onion, garlic, and tomatoes in the oil until onions are soft. Then add the beef and pork and continue cooking until the meat is done. Remove from heat. Add the cilantro and season to taste. Assemble the tacos, meat first, and toppings in the order they are listed.

Makes 12 tacos

TEXAS GRILLED STEAK NACHOS

We've all seen the paper basket of three-week-old store-bought corn chips topped with canned cheese and jalapeño rings at the ball game. If that's your idea of nachos, this fantastic recipe will change your mind forever. These Grilled Steak Nachos are so tasty that your guests will beg for more.

Nachos, like many great dishes, were conceived out of necessity. Back in 1943, a guy by the name of Ignacio Anaya was working at the Victory Club in Piedras Negras, Mexico, just across the border from Eagle Pass, Texas. A group of officers' wives, whose husbands were stationed at Fort Duncan Air Base, had come across the border for dinner. Señor Anaya couldn't find the cook, so he went into the kitchen, put some grated Wisconsin cheddar on tostadas (fried corn tortillas), popped them under the broiler, and then, once the cheese melted, topped them with a slice of jalapeño. The name of the snack, Nachos Especiales, was later shortened to "nachos," after Ignacio. This Tex-Mex version includes a bite of grilled steak. Enjoy!

1 (1-pound) rib-eye steak, mesquite-grilled to medium rare, seasoned to taste with salt and pepper, and then cut into small slices

6 corn tortillas, quartered

Oil for deep-frying

2 cups (about ½ pound) grated Monterey Jack cheese

3 jalapeño peppers, sliced into thin rings

¼ bunch cilantro, chopped

¼ white onion, chopped

1 Roma tomato, chopped

½ avocado, chopped

½ cup sour cream

Deep-fry the tortilla quarters to a golden brown, drain on a paper towel, and salt immediately. Arrange the fried tortillas on a baking sheet and top with the cheese, steak, and then jalapeños. Place in a 325-degree oven for 5 to 8 minutes or until the cheese is fully melted. Top with cilantro, onion, tomato, avocado, and small dollops of sour cream.

Serves 6 as an appetizer

To douse the heat from chiles, try dairy products like milk, cheese, yogurt or ice cream. Water and beer only spread the heat!

SAN ANTONIO–STYLE GOAT CHEESE ENCHILADAS

These delicious goat cheese enchiladas offer an ancho enchilada sauce that uses tomatoes. You'd never find this combination in authentic Mexican cooking. However, this blending of readily available ingredients is an everyday practice in this well-developed style of cooking.

Tex-Mex Ancho Enchilada Sauce:

5 ancho chilies

3 tablespoons canola oil

½ white onion, chopped fine

3 cloves garlic, chopped fine

½ cup dry white wine

1 (14-ounce) can plum tomatoes, pureed

2 cups chicken broth

2 teaspoons ground cumin

1 teaspoon Mexican oregano

Salt and freshly ground pepper

Goat Cheese Enchilada Filling:

1¼ pounds goat cheese

3 cloves garlic, chopped

¼ cup freshly grated Pecorino Romano cheese

Salt and freshly ground pepper

¼ cup finely chopped cilantro

12 corn tortillas

8 ounces Monterey Jack cheese, grated

Garnish:

¼ cup chopped cilantro

Avocado Sour Cream (page 61)

Chopped green onions

Remove the stems and seeds from the ancho chiles. Place the chiles in a bowl and just cover with boiling water. Set aside to soften for 15 minutes. Place the chiles and 1/4 cup of the soaking liquid in a blender or food processor and puree until smooth. (Be careful—hot liquids can expand in a blender.)

In a medium saucepan, sauté the onions and garlic in the oil until soft. Work the ancho paste through a wire sieve into the saucepan with the back of a rubber spatula. Add wine, tomatoes, chicken broth, cumin, and oregano; simmer uncovered for 25 to 30 minutes or until slightly thickened. Season to taste with salt and pepper.

To make the filling, place goat cheese, garlic, and Pecorino Romano in a food processor and process until smooth. Season with salt and pepper, and stir in the cilantro.

Spread 1/2 cup of the Ancho Enchilada Sauce into a medium baking dish. Dip tortillas one at a time in remaining Ancho Enchilada Sauce to lightly coat both sides. Spoon about 2 tablespoons of Goat Cheese Filling in the center of each tortilla, then roll it up and place it in the baking dish, seam side down. The tortillas should fit snugly together. Pour the remaining Ancho Enchilada sauce over the enchiladas and top with the grated Monterey Jack cheese.

Bake in a preheated 350-degree oven for 30 minutes or until the enchiladas are hot at the center and the cheese has fully melted. Remove and garnish with a sprinkle of chopped cilantro, a dollop of Avocado Sour Cream, and chopped green onions.

Makes 12 enchiladas

WEST TEXAS MESQUITE-SMOKED BRISKET OF BEEF

Mesquite smoking is a true American art form. I've had so many good meals ruined by amateurs trying to add a smoky flavor to their barbecue by using mesquite wood or even the chips. My advice is to use Mesquite chunk charcoal. It burns hot and never overpowers. Since you are looking for "low and slow" when smoking meats—that's low temperature and slow cooking—chunk charcoal is the foolproof choice.

1 whole brisket

1 batch West Texas Barbecue Rub (page 68)

1 batch West Texas Flaming Mop Sauce
   (page 68)

Rub the brisket thoroughly with the Barbecue Rub and let stand at room temperature for 1 hour. Place the brisket in the smoker fat side up and close the lid. Light a few chunks of charcoal and bring the temperature in the smoker to somewhere between 190 degrees and 220 degrees. Smoke the brisket for a minimum of 8 and as many as 10 hours, turning every 2 to 3 hours. When the brisket is done, slice thin and serve on French bread with West Texas Flaming Mop Sauce on the side.

Serves 10 to 12

WEST TEXAS BARBECUE RUB

This is called a rub for a reason. You need to rub it into the meat. I like it best rubbed in and then wrapped in plastic film and rested over night. This rule doesn't apply to fish. Heck, you can just sprinkle it on fish.

6 tablespoons ancho chile powder or mild New Mexico chile powder

1 tablespoon sugar

3 tablespoons brown sugar

3 tablespoons kosher salt

2 tablespoons freshly ground coarse black pepper

1 tablespoon ground cumin

1 tablespoon cayenne pepper

Mix and store in a covered container.

Makes about 1 cup

WEST TEXAS FLAMING MOP SAUCE

For those of you who are just learning about barbecue, this is an important day in your life. Barbecue sauce is used to cover up the flavor of inferior cuts of meat, or to enhance great barbecue by sitting on the side as an accent. Mopping sauce is a completely different animal. Its purpose is to tenderize while flavorizing. The rule of thumb for brisket and ribs is "low and slow." While smoking the meat, give it a little mop every 20 minutes or so. You'll see and taste the difference the first time you try it!

1¾ cups white vinegar

3 tablespoons Louisiana hot sauce

1 teaspoon sugar

1 tablespoon dark brown sugar

1 teaspoon cayenne pepper

1 teaspoon kosher salt

1 teaspoon freshly ground black pepper

Mix in a nonreactive bowl and cover. Mop onto ribs, pork shoulder, or brisket while slow smoking.

Makes about 2 cups

DOWN-HOME SPICY CABBAGE

This is the type of side dish that defines Southern cooking. Simple and easy to prepare, and the flavor is unbelievable. Next to my Texas-Style "Chicken Shack" Fried Chicken (page 56), it's a slice of "Lone Star Heaven."

½ pound hardwood-smoked bacon

1 large head green cabbage, cored and
chopped

5 scallions, chopped

2 cloves garlic, minced

1 teaspoon crushed red chile

1 teaspoon salt

½ teaspoon freshly ground black pepper

⅓ cup water

In large heavy frying pan or Dutch oven, fry the bacon until crisp. Remove the bacon from the pan and crumble. Drain all but 1 table-spoon of the drippings from the pan. Place the cabbage and the bacon back in the pan. Add all other ingredients, cover, and cook over medium heat for 5 minutes. Stir, reduce heat, and simmer for 20 minutes or until cabbage is fully cooked.

Serves 6 to 8

Mrs. Lady Bird Johnson, wife of the president, had cards printed with LBJ's chili recipe. She was quoted as saying, "It has been almost as popular as the government pamphlet on the care and feeding of children."

SPICY COLLARD GREENS

Years ago my dad took me to a soul-food restaurant in Phoenix. The place was very clean, but on each table was a little bottle of Trappy's peppers. The bottles were so old that the labels were half worn off. I asked my dad about the peppers and he said the peppers weren't for eating. He went on to explain that every night the owner fills up these bottles with white vinegar. And every day his customers come in and drizzle the vinegar over the greens. Greens are delicious, but add a little pepper vinegar and they come alive with flavor.

2 tablespoons olive oil

½ white onion, chopped fine

2 cloves garlic

½ pound smoked ham hocks

2 teaspoons salt

1 teaspoon crushed red chile

1 teaspoon black pepper

1 teaspoon paprika

1 tablespoon hot red pepper sauce

1 large bunch collard greens

1 tablespoon butter

In a large stockpot, sauté the onion and garlic in the oil until soft but not browned. Add 3 quarts of water and bring to a boil. Add ham hocks, spices, and hot sauce. Reduce heat to low and simmer for 1 hour. Wash the collard greens thoroughly. Remove the stems from the center of the larger leaves. The stems of the smaller leaves are tender and don't need to be removed. Tear the greens into 1/2-inch thick strips. Place greens in the stockpot with the ham hock and add the butter. Simmer for 1 hour, stirring occasionally. Check to make sure the greens are tender, adjust seasoning, and serve with white vinegar.

Serves 4 to 6

TEXAS-STYLE BLACK-EYED PEAS

One of the things I love about eating down South is that people don't shy away from the foods that their grandparents loved. Traditional dishes like this one are held in high esteem and passed down to the next generation. Make these tonight; you might just start a new tradition at your house.

1 tablespoon canola oil

½ white onion, chopped

2 cloves garlic, minced

½ green bell pepper, chopped

½ teaspoon turmeric

1 teaspoon cayenne pepper

1 (14-ounce) can diced tomatoes, drained

½ teaspoon cumin

1 (14-ounce) can black-eyed peas, undrained

1 tablespoon freshly squeezed lemon juice

Sauté the onion, garlic, bell pepper, turmeric, and cayenne in the oil for 2 to 3 minutes. Add tomatoes and cumin and cook for 5 minutes more. Then add black-eyed peas (and a little water if needed). Simmer for 15 minutes. Stir in lemon juice. Serve over white rice.

Serves 4 to 6

TEX-MEX-STYLE PICO DE GALLO

Pico de gallo *means "beak of a rooster," which refers to the biting sharp heat that this salsa often has. This is basic Tex-Mex salsa for nachos, tacos, or hot corn chips!*

2 whole jalapeño chiles, diced

½ white onion, diced

3 large ripe Roma tomatoes, diced

½ bunch fresh cilantro, chopped

2 teaspoons corn oil

½ teaspoon salt

Juice of ½ key lime

Mix all ingredients together and let stand 1 hour to blend.

Makes 2½ cups

Will Rogers (1879–1935), popular humorist and actor, called chili "a bowl of blessedness." After keeping a written score on chili in hundreds of towns scattered throughout Texas and Oklahoma, he decided that the world's finest chili came from a small café in Coleman, Texas.

STRAWBERRY SHORTCAKE WITH AMARETTO CARAMEL SAUCE

I thought you might like something to cool down your burning tongue. Everybody loves strawberry shortcake. This delicious caramel sauce puts it in a class all by itself.

6 cups fresh strawberries

1 cup sugar

Shortcakes:

1 cup flour

3 tablespoons sugar

1½ teaspoons baking powder

⅛ teaspoon table salt

¼ teaspoon freshly grated nutmeg

2 tablespoons sweet butter, cut into pieces

1 lightly beaten egg

¼ cup heavy cream

Amaretto Caramel Sauce:

2 tablespoons sweet butter

⅓ cup light brown sugar

2 tablespoons Amaretto

1 tablespoon heavy cream

Finish:

½ cup heavy cream

Remove the stems from the strawberries and cut berries in half. Place them in a glass bowl and stir in the sugar. Cover with plastic and put in the refrigerator for 1/2 hour.

Preheat the oven to 400 degrees. Sift flour, sugar, baking powder, salt, and nutmeg in a medium bowl and stir well. Add butter and work mixture with a pastry cutter or 2 knives until dough resembles a coarse meal. Mix egg and cream together; stir into dough just until it holds together. Drop the dough a spoonful at a time onto a greased cookie sheet and bake for about 10 minutes or until golden on top. When biscuits are done, place on a wire rack and allow them to cool.

For caramel sauce, stir the butter, brown sugar, Amaretto, and cream together in a medium saucepan. Bring to a low boil over medium heat. Remove from heat and keep warm.

To assemble the dessert, cut biscuit in half, place bottom half in the bottom of a shallow bowl. Spoon strawberries and their juice over bottom half of the biscuit and cover with the top half. Spoon Amaretto Caramel Sauce over the biscuit and berries, and then pour a little cream around outside of finished shortcake.

Makes 6

MARGARITA

If you think margaritas are a Mexican drink, you're wrong. The true history of the margarita (like so many things in Texas) depends on whom you're talking with. The most popular story tells that the margarita was invented in Acapulco, Mexico, by a rich socialite from Dallas named Margarita Sames. At a Christmas party Margarita was behind the bar making up drinks for her rich friends when she came up with the now-famous concoction. Everyone liked it so much they took the recipe home to Texas and the popularity of the drink spread like wildfire. Then tourists in Mexico asked for the supposed Mexican drink, causing it to spread there. In fact, Mexicans think of margaritas as a tourist drink.

1½ shots tequila reposado

1½ shots Cointreau

Juice of 1 key lime

Shake with ice and serve.

Serves 1

RED ROOSTER

This is for those Sunday mornings when you wake up a little fuzzy—as they say, "The hair of the dog that bit you!"

⅓ cup Bloody Mary mix

1 ice-cold bottle Lone Star Beer

1 pickled jalapeño pepper, with a few slits
  cut in the side

1 pair of dark sunglasses

Pour the Bloody Mary mix in a chilled beer mug and slowly top it off with the beer. Garnish with the jalapeño. Put on the sunglasses and sip slowly.

Serves 1

American outlaw and legend Jesse James (1847–1882) once refused to rob a bank in McKinney, Texas, because that's where his favorite chili parlor was located.

WEST TEXAS SLAMMER

Around my house we keep the tequila in the freezer, the bottom third of the bottle frozen in a block of ice. The tequila comes out of the bottle thick and viscous, and is so much sweeter than if it's stored in a hot cupboard. I learned this trick while I was a guest of the Cuervo Company in Mexico. If you are going to make West Texas Slammers, it's best to use tequila that is as cold as you can get it . . . and give someone your car keys.

1½ ounces ice-cold Jose Cuervo Traditional
   Tequila
Dash of Tabasco Habanero Sauce
Splash of club soda

Pour the tequila and Tabasco in a small bar glass. Pour in a little club soda. Put one hand over the top of the glass and slam it down on the bar. Then slam it down your throat while its still fizzing. So the order is: slam the slammer, and then slam the slammer . . . a process that, when repeated, has landed many a Texan in the local slammer!

Serves 1

CATHOLICS

AS WE SAY GOODBYE TO TEXAS, we cross the Rio Grande into the land of enchantment. In order to discuss the food here, we need to stop for a minute while I get one of my pet peeves off my chest. Who has the best Mexican food—Arizona or New Mexico? I have had at least a hundred discussions on this subject. And it's always with someone who tells me they prefer the Mexican food in New Mexico. Here's the news: "It is hard to find good Mexican food in New Mexico!"

What New Mexico has is "New Mexican food," which is fantastic, but in reality only a distant cousin to the many different styles of food found down in Mexico. New Mexican food is a combination of Spanish, Native American, and Central American cuisines with a Mexican influence. But since New Mexico has been basically self-sufficient for the last five hundred years, this is a separately developed, independent cuisine. New Mexico can boast that they have been cooking with chiles and developing chile-related cuisine longer than any other area in the U.S.

Modern-day New Mexican cooking finds its roots in the pre-Columbian peoples of Central America. Their diet was centered around corn, beans, squash, and chiles. Both the Incan and Mayan people grew several varieties of chiles. There is a debate as to whether the Pueblo Indians and their ancestors grew chiles or only harvested them in the wild. It is believed that they traded chile seeds, among other things, with a Central American group known as the Pochteca for centuries before Spain and the Catholic Church set up shop in the New World. There is an erroneous account that the founder of Santa Fe, a captain-general by the name of Juan de Oñate, introduced chile peppers north of what is now the Mexican border in 1598. However, the Spanish, being expansionist, surely increased production. Catholic priests were known for collecting and carrying chile seeds on their travels and cultivating them along the way.

Regardless of which version is true, by the early 1600s there were Catholic settlements all through the area we now call New Mexico. Although the natives had been harvesting the wild chiles that grow in southern New Mexico (most likely the chile tepin), the missionaries and settlers started growing new varieties like the jalapeño, serrano, poblano, and the ancestor of what we now call the New Mexico chile.

The New Mexico chile is the dominant chile category in this region. I say category because there are so many chile varieties that fall under the name New Mexican. Oddly enough, one of the best known is the Anaheim, which was developed in California in the early twentieth century from seeds collected in New Mexico. (By the way, Anaheim, California, is not known for chile production.) Other varieties include Big Jim, Española Improved, Sandia, and the New Mexico 6–4.

acres of green chiles under cultivation. Most chiles grown in Hatch are used in New Mexico. Some have suggested that many "Hatch green chiles" are grown as far away as southeastern Arizona. There is no specific variety by the name of Hatch; instead, there are several New Mexican varieties grown throughout the Mesilla Valley. It's one of the great chile-growing

The most popular choice of chile farmers is the New Mexico 6–4.

The most popular choice of chile farmers is the New Mexico 6–4. With its mild heat of 3–4, it is harvested when green for green chile, or it's allowed to mature to a deep red color and then dried and ground for red chile powder.

New Mexico is the home of the world-famous Hatch green chile, which is enjoyed the world over . . . or is it? Hatch has a wonderful climate for growing chiles, but it has only a few hundred

regions in the world. The green chiles grown at this higher altitude are hotter than similar varieties grown in Texas and California. The thing I like about the resulting food in New Mexico is it's delicious, simple, and hot—in fact, very hot—which they don't warn you about or apologize for!

In the late 1980s, the nation's desire for hot and spicy foods was on the rise. In Albuquerque a chile-head food writer saw the growing trend and wisely responded. Dave DeWitt and his cowriter on many a project, Nancy Gerlach, started *Chile Pepper* magazine. Their first issue had 212 subscribers; by 1995 the magazine had over 50,000, with a total circulation of more than 80,000. In 1990 Dave started *The Fiery Foods Show,* and overnight small producers of chile-related products had a national platform not only to market their wares but also to meet and work with their competition head-on. They could go to the show and meet any-

authorities on chiles. He has published thirty-one books on the subject and is working on number thirty-two. He has appeared on many national television series and has been featured in the *New Yorker, New York Times, Los Angeles Times, USA Today, American Way, Smithsonian,* and in hundreds of other newspapers. Since 1996 Dave has published *Fiery Foods and Barbecue Business Magazine.* He is so well known in the chile community that he is referred to as "The Pepper Pope." Dave is one of many

Dave DeWitt is so well known in the chile community that he is referred to as "The Pepper Pope."

one, from a "hot shop" owner in Quebec, to a specialty food distributor for the East Coast. Dave, who has a master's degree in literature and is a board member of the Chile Pepper Institute at New Mexico University, is one of the world's leading

food/chile writers who has written about Sister Mary of Agreda. Back in 1960 George and Bertha Herter not only told the story in their book *Bull Cook and Authentic Historical Recipes and Practices,* they also claimed to have Sister Maria's original recipe! (I can't help but wonder if the Herters were from Texas.)

In 1618, at age sixteen, a Catholic girl named Sister Maria, who lived at a con-"Chile con Carne" (page 89). From Maria's description of the region, the Catholic Church felt she may have been talking about the American Southwest.

A good bowl of New Mexico chile, red or green, is somehow heaven-sent.

vent in Agreda, Spain, reportedly went into metaphysical trances in which her sprit traveled to a far-off land. When questioned by her superiors, she told of an arid climate and a native people that she had taught about Christ. She reported telling the natives to seek out Catholic missionaries for conversion and baptism. This was so extraordinary that Maria was brought before the Holy Inquisition to determine if these visions were indeed real or if she was a heretic. She fully described the land, people, daily life, and food. One dish she reported was a mixture of meat and chiles, hence the name

The Church had portraits of Maria painted and sent to the New World. In the Americas the missionaries started showing the portraits. The Jumanos, a group of natives from Tejas, which is east of Albuquerque, told the missionaries that she was indeed the Blue Lady, or Dama de Azul. She had appeared from time to time to help them and was the one who first taught them about Christ and baptism.

Whether you believe this tale or not, it supports what I've know all my life—a good bowl of New Mexico chile, red or green, is somehow heaven-sent.

...XICO GREEN CHILE WITH PORK

...nk about the Southwest, this is the first dish that comes to mind. It's very hot but, oh, so ...You can find it served all day long in one form or another. You haven't lived until you've ...reakfast of eggs and Green Chile with Pork!

...immed and cut into
bite-size pieces

1 white onion, chopped

4 cloves fresh garlic, minced

1 tablespoon corn oil

1 (48-ounce) can chicken broth

4 pounds hot New Mexico green chiles,
   roasted, peeled, and chopped

2 teaspoons Mexican oregano

1 tablespoon ground cumin   *½ tsp*

Salt to taste

Black pepper to taste

In a large Dutch oven, sauté the onions and garlic in the oil until soft but not browned. Set aside. Brown the pork and then add the onion-and-garlic mixture, chicken broth, and roasted chiles. Bring to a boil, reduce heat, and simmer for about 1 hour *3 hrs*. Add spices and season to taste. If stew gets too thick while cooking, add a little water. Stir often. Serve with warm corn tortillas in big soup bowls.

Serves 8

Double recipe!

20 Anaheim chiles + 4 jalapenos for double recipe.
Leave spices the same but double everything else. Simmer partially covered for 3 hours. Keep boiled water on stove to add if necessary. Poach eggs in sauce!

Ristras

Ristras—dried chiles strung together and seen hanging in households throughout New Mexico—are an age-old symbol of welcome. They are also thought to ward off evils! You see them printed on everything New Mexican, from oven mitts and T-shirts to wind socks and coffee cups. Did you know that chiles are the official vegetable of New Mexico?

SPICY SAGE AND BEER-BRINED PORK LOIN

Using Mexican beer, red chile, brown sugar, and molasses in this marinade adds a depth of flavor. Combine that with the slow spit roasting and—Wow!—that's the way roasted pork was meant to be eaten.

5 cups hot water

½ cup dark brown sugar

½ cup kosher salt

8 to 10 cloves garlic, chopped

2 tablespoons dark molasses

1 tablespoon freshly ground black pepper

1 tablespoon crushed red chile

2 teaspoons dried sage

2 teaspoons Dijon mustard

1 or 2 drops liquid smoke

3 bottles cold Negra Modelo or your favorite dark beer

1 (3-pound) boneless pork loin, excess fat trimmed

In a large nonreactive bowl whisk together the hot water, brown sugar, and salt until fully dissolved. Whisk in the garlic, molasses, pepper, red chile, sage, mustard, and liquid smoke. Then stir in the beer. Refrigerate the brine for 1 hour, and then place the pork loin in the brine. Set a plate on top to keep the loin submerged. Marinate for 24 hours.

Spit-roast the pork until it reaches an internal temperature of 160 degrees. Allow to rest for 10 minutes before slicing.

Serves 8 to 10

GRILL-ROASTED DOUBLE-THICK PORK CHOPS WITH POBLANOS, PARSNIPS, AND PEARS

Juicy delicious pork chops every time. Who could ask for more?

4 double-thick pork chops

1 batch Tangy Rosemary-Lemon Marinade
   for Pork or Lamb (see below)

3 poblano chiles, roasted, peeled, and
   chopped

3 pears, cut lengthwise into quarters and
   cored

3 parsnips, cut in half and quartered
   lengthwise

½ pound baby red potatoes

½ pound baby white potatoes

Salt and freshly ground black pepper
   to taste

Marinate the pork chops in the marinade from 3 to 5 hours. Place the marinade and pork along with the poblanos, pears, parsnips, and potatoes in a roasting pan and toss well to coat. Season with salt and pepper and bake in a preheated 425-degree oven for about 1 hour or until the chops are 165 degrees at the center of the thickest part. Serve immediately.

Serves 4

TANGY ROSEMARY-LEMON MARINADE FOR PORK OR LAMB

6 to 8 sprigs fresh rosemary, bruised

5 cloves fresh garlic, smashed

½ cup olive oil

3 thick-sliced fresh lemons, squeezed
   into the marinade

1 teaspoon crushed red chile

Fresh black pepper to taste

In a nonreactive bowl, toss all ingredients together including the lemon peel. Marinate pork or lamb for up to 5 hours.

Makes 3½ cups marinade

ADOVADA

...marinated in adobo sauce—this is an often-overlooked dish on menus throughout the ...west. It has a rich, delicious taste followed with a burning fire. It's an old family favorite.

...ico red chile pods
6 cu... broth
3 cloves garlic, minced
2 teaspoons Mexican oregano
2 teaspoons ground cumin
½ teaspoon cayenne pepper
1 teaspoon salt
4- to 5-pound boneless pork shoulder
¼ cup canola oil

Remove stems, seeds, and veins from the chiles. Carefully toast the pods in a dry iron frying pan until soft and pliable but not burnt (if the chiles burn they will become bitter). Simmer the chiles in the chicken broth along with the garlic, oregano, cumin, cayenne pepper, and salt for 20 minutes. Run chiles and broth through the blender 1/2 cup at a time. (Be careful—hot liquids expand in a blender and can spill over the top and burn you.) Work sauce through a wire sieve with the back of a spoon into a mixing bowl until only the chile solids are left in the sieve; discard these.

Trim any excess fat from the pork roast and cut into large chunks. Brown the pork in a Dutch oven, and then cover with the chile sauce. Cover and bake at 325 degrees for 1 1/2 hours. Remove from oven, let cool enough to handle, shred pork with two forks, and mix back into sauce. Serve with hot corn tortillas and ice-cold beer.

Serves 10 to 12

Mexican folk remedies for removing the heat from your hands after handling chiles include washing with honey and scrubbing with coarse salt before rinsing!

CHILE CON CARNE MARY OF AGREDA

This is reputed to be a version of the first written recipe for Chile con Carne.

2 pounds venison or antelope

1 pound fresh javelina

2 tablespoons antelope fat

1 (2-inch-diameter) onion, chopped fine

4 cloves garlic, chopped fine

3 level tablespoons water

3 bay leaves

1 quart ripe tomatoes

1 cup chile pepper pulp

1 level tablespoon oregano

1 level teaspoon cumin

1 level tablespoon salt

Cut the meat into 1/2-inch-square cubes. Melt the antelope fat in a large covered pot. Dice the onion and garlic and brown them in the fat. Add meat and water; cover and steam well for 5 minutes.

Rub the tomatoes through a colander and add to meat. Stir in the chile pepper pulp, add the bay leaves, and cook for 20 minutes. Now add the oregano, cumin, and salt and cook slowly for about 2 hours. Add a little water to keep from burning, but add as little as possible.

Serves 10 to 12

XICO RED POSOLÉ

classic Native American dish from New Mexico. You'll find versions of it anywhere in the
est where chiles and corn grow. We always make it at Christmas or on a cold winter day.
our house, winter would not be winter without a steaming hot bowl of posolé!

ico red chile pods

2 (4... ..ans chicken broth

4 cloves fresh garlic, minced

1 teaspoon ground cumin

1 teaspoon whole Mexican oregano

2 tablespoons corn oil

2 pounds roasted pork, cut into chunks

2 (28-ounce) cans white hominy, drained

Garnish:

¼ purple cabbage, shredded

1 bunch fresh cilantro, washed and
chopped fine

½ white onion, chopped fine

1 bunch red radishes, washed and thinly
sliced

1 tablespoon chile tepins

2 fresh key limes, cut into wedges

Remove stems, seeds, and veins from the chiles. Carefully toast the pods in a dry iron frying pan until soft and pliable but not burnt (if the chiles burn they will become bitter). Simmer the chiles in the chicken broth along with the garlic, cumin, and oregano for 20 minutes. Run chiles and broth through the blender, 1/2 cup at a time. (Be careful—hot liquids expand in a blender and can spill over the top and burn you.) Work the broth and chiles through a wire sieve with the back of a spoon into a mixing bowl until only the chile solids are left in the sieve; discard these.

In a stockpot, brown the pork in oil, and then add chile/chicken broth mixture and hominy. Simmer on low for a few hours. (I let it burble along all day; it makes the house smell great!) Stir occasionally. Serve in big soup bowls topped with purple cabbage, white onion, radish slices, and cilantro. Crush 1 chile tepin on top and drizzle with a squeeze of fresh lime.

Serves 8

NEW MEXICO LAMB AND CHICOS STEW

This is a traditional Native American stew made throughout the Southwest. It uses chicos, which are dried corn kernels that have been roasted in an horno, *or adobe oven. Making this wonderful stew takes several hours so we always start in the morning on a cold winter day. By noon the house is full of the enticing aroma, the stew is ready, and so are we. Chicos can be purchased at many southwestern gift shops in New Mexico or through the mail.*

1 pound chicos

5 cups water

5 cups chicken broth

1 tablespoon corn oil

1 white onion, chopped

3 cloves garlic, chopped fine

1 pound lamb stew meat, cut into 1-inch
   cubes

4 or 5 fresh Anaheim, Hatch, or poblano
   chiles, roasted, peeled, deveined, seeded,
   and chopped

Salt and pepper to taste

Place the chicos in a large stockpot with the water and chicken broth, and bring to a rolling boil. Reduce heat to simmer, cover, and cook for 2 1/2 to 3 hours.

When time is up, heat the oil over medium heat in a large Dutch oven or heavy pot. Sauté the onion until soft. Add the garlic and continue cooking for 30 seconds. Add the lamb meat and sauté until well browned. Ladle some of the hot liquid from the chicos into the Dutch oven. Deglaze the pan by working brown bits lose from the bottom of the pan into the stew with a rubber spatula. Add all of the chicos and liquid to the lamb. Bring to a boil, cover, reduce heat to low, and simmer for another hour. Then add the chiles, simmer for 15 minutes more, taste, and season. Serve in big soup bowls with warm bread or tortillas.

Serves 6 to 8

Central American Indian tribes strung chiles together and tied them to their canoes to ward off evils lurking in the water.

GRILL-ROASTED POBLANO CORN CHOWDER

In late August, when the fresh ripe corn is being picked, we always make a batch of this wonderful soup. It's one of the few dishes that is so good, I serve it alone.

4 ears of sweet corn, cleaned and lightly oiled

4 slices of hardwood-smoked bacon, cut into bite-size pieces

1 large red bell pepper, diced

1 white onion, diced

¼ cup all-purpose flour

5 cups warm chicken stock

2 cups peeled and diced russet potatoes

2 poblano chiles, roasted, peeled, seeded, and cut into strips

1 bay leaf

2 tablespoons sweet butter

½ cup cream

2 teaspoons brown sugar

½ teaspoon Worcestershire sauce

¼ teaspoon Tabasco Sauce

2 tablespoons finely chopped Italian parsley

Salt and pepper to taste

Toss the corn on the grill until lightly browned; allow it to cool.

Meanwhile, fry the bacon over medium heat until crisp, about 10 minutes. Add the red bell pepper and onion and sauté until soft, about 6 minutes.

Cut the kernels from the cobs with a sharp knife and scrape the cobs into a bowl, releasing and saving the milky liquid. Save the corncobs. Puree half of the corn along with the milky liquid in a food processor. As soon as the bell peppers and onion are soft, sprinkle in the flour and fry for a few minutes. Whisk in the chicken stock and then add all the corn, the cobs, potatoes, chiles, and bay leaf. Bring to a simmer for 20 minutes or until potatoes are soft; stir occasionally to prevent corn from sticking. Remove corncobs and bay leaf, add all other ingredients, stir well, and season. Serve immediately.

Serves 6

CHILE RELLENOS

In New Mexico, chile rellenos are serious business. If you want to start an argument in Albuquerque, just ask who makes the best one.

15 Hatch or Anaheim green chiles with
    stems
¾ pound muenster, Monterey Jack, or
    queso oaxaca
All-purpose flour
8 eggs
½ teaspoon cream of tartar
Pinch of salt
Corn oil for frying
Salt

Roast the skin of the chiles over the flame of a gas burner, the grill, or under the broiler until the entire exterior is blistered and brown. Place the chiles in a plastic or paper bag, squeeze out the air, and then fold the bag down. Let the chiles stand for 10 minutes, and then peel them. Cut a small slit in the side of the chiles and remove the seedpod and excess seeds. Put 1 to 2 tablespoons of cheese inside the slit of each chile. Dredge the chiles in flour. In a large Dutch oven, heat the oil to 350 degrees.

Separate the eggs and lightly beat the yolks with a fork. In a food processor, beat the whites and the cream of tarter with a little salt until very stiff. Gently fold in the beaten yolks with a rubber spatula.

Pick up one chile at a time by the stem, dip in egg batter, and very carefully set it in the hot oil with tongs. When golden brown on one side, carefully turn it and brown the other side. Remove from oil, place on a paper towel to drain, salt lightly, and serve immediately.

Serves 15

"Wish I had time for just one more bowl of chili."
Alleged dying words of Kit Carson (1809–1868)

TOMATILLO SALSA

A real New Mexican treat. You'll see this topping chicken enchiladas. It's great with any roasted pork or poultry, and I love it with huevos rancheros.

1 pound tomatillos, husks removed, washed well

2 whole serrano chiles

2 cloves garlic, chopped

1 tablespoon corn oil

⅓ cup chicken broth

Salt to taste

In a medium saucepan, barely cover the tomatillos and chiles with water and simmer for 8 minutes or until tomatillos turn soft. Transfer tomatillos, chiles, and 1/4 cup of cooking water to a blender; add garlic and blend until smooth.

In a large heavy frying pan, heat oil over medium heat, add tomatillo mixture, and simmer for 5 minutes, stirring occasionally. Add chicken broth and continue to cook for 5 minutes more. Salt to taste.

Makes 2 cups

NAVAJO TACOS

On the Navajo reservation in the Four Corners region, you can buy these delicious tacos. It's a cross between fry bread and an open-faced burrito. They're messy but worth it!

3 cups all-purpose flour

1 tablespoon baking powder

½ teaspoon salt

1½ cups warm water

Oil for frying

1½ cups red chile or Carne Adovada (page 88)

1 cup shredded cheddar cheese

2 cups shredded lettuce

1 cup chopped tomatoes

½ cup roasted green chiles

½ cup chopped white onion

Mix flour, baking powder, and salt in a large bowl. Add warm water and stir until dough begins to form a ball. On a lightly floured surface knead dough, but do not overwork. Place kneaded dough in a bowl covered with plastic wrap, and refrigerate for 1 hour.

Heat oil to 350 degrees in a Dutch oven or deep frying pan. Lightly flour a working surface and pat out baseball-sized circles of dough. Cut holes in middles with a knife; this helps the dough to fry flat. Carefully set the dough in the hot oil and cook until golden brown, then flip and cook other side until golden brown. Cooking takes about 3 minutes. Drain on paper towel.

Top freshly made Indian fry bread with red chile and cheese, and then top with lettuce, tomatoes, green chiles, and onion.

Makes 6

NEW MEXICO–STYLE RED CHILE CHEESE ENCHILADAS

If you're used to eating Tex-Mex, you're in for a surprise when ordering enchiladas in New Mexico. The enchiladas come flat, stacked up like pancakes, with layers of cheese and onion in between. Then they are topped with fried eggs and served this way for breakfast, lunch, or dinner! The thing that makes them so special is the Red Chile Enchilada Sauce. Serve them with pinto beans and ice-cold beer. You won't be disappointed!

12 corn tortillas

2 cups Mild New Mexico–Style Red Chile Enchilada Sauce, heated (see below)

2 cups shredded Monterey Jack cheese

1 cup chopped white onion

8 eggs

2 cups shredded lettuce

1 large tomato, chopped

Dip a tortilla in the sauce and place on a dinner plate. Top that with 2 heaping tablespoons shredded cheese and 1 tablespoon onion, and then pour 2 tablespoons of the Red Chile Enchilada Sauce over that. Repeat this process two more times. Prepare 3 more plates in the same manner. Heat the enchiladas in the oven or under the broiler until cheese melts.

Meanwhile, fry the eggs to your liking. Remove enchiladas from the oven and top with the two fried eggs. Garnish plate with lettuce and tomato.

Serves 4

MILD NEW MEXICO–STYLE RED CHILE ENCHILADA SAUCE

You'll never look at canned enchilada sauce the same after one bit of this wonderful sauce!

10 to 12 dried mild New Mexico red chile pods

4 cups chicken broth

2 cloves garlic, minced

1½ teaspoons dried Mexican oregano

1 teaspoon ground cumin

½ teaspoon kosher salt

½ teaspoon brown sugar

Roast the chiles on a hot comal or in a frying pan until soft and pliable. Remove chiles from comal and allow to cool a little. Remove stems and seeds. Place all ingredients in a saucepan and simmer for 15 minutes. Pour in a blender, 3/4 cup at a time, and puree. (Be careful—hot liquids expand in a blender and can spill over the top and burn you.) Pour the sauce through a sieve and mash with the back of a spoon, working until only the coarse solids are left; discard these. If sauce is too thin, simmer to reduce. Serve warm with New Mexico–Style Red Chile Cheese Enchiladas.

Makes 5 cups

NEW MEXICO GREEN CHILE SAUCE

"Red or green?" the waitress asks. So the customer says, "Well, which is hotter?" She emphatically replies, "The green!" This conversation happens hundreds (if not thousands) of times a day throughout the Southwest. The two basic sauces are served on rellenos, enchiladas, tamales, eggs, and the list goes on. This is a quick and easy recipe for basic green chile sauce. When I make this, I like to use a mixture of chiles in the sauce. Make a big batch; it freezes well.

16 New Mexico, Hatch, Anaheim, or
    poblano chiles
3 cups chicken broth
4 or 5 cloves garlic, minced
1 teaspoon salt (omit if using canned
    chicken broth)

Using tongs, roast the chiles over an open flame or on a gas grill, turning until they are totally blistered and dark brown. Remove the chiles from the heat and place them in a small paper sack or plastic bag. Fold the top down to hold the heat inside. After ten minutes remove chiles from the bag. Wearing rubber gloves, run the chiles under cold water and remove the skin. It will come off easily. Then tear out the stem and seedpod at the center of the chile and discard. Remove any white veins.

Run the chiles and all other ingredients through the blender or food processor until they form a thick puree. If using within 6 or 7 days, just pop the sauce in the refrigerator. When ready to use, bring to a simmer and serve.

Make 4 cups

JALAPEÑO BACON CORNBREAD

It's cornbread with an attitude! We like to clean out the refrigerator when making cornbread. Cheese, chiles, veggies . . . they all go in the cornbread!

2½ cups cornmeal

1 cup all-purpose flour

2 tablespoons baking powder

½ cup brown sugar

1 teaspoon salt

2 cups buttermilk

1 cup medium cheddar cheese, grated

1 cup frozen corn, thawed

½ pound bacon, fried, drained, and crumbled

⅓ cup butter, melted

3 jalapeño chiles (seeds removed), diced

2 eggs

Mix all dry ingredients together with a fork. Then add all other ingredients and mix well. Pour into a lightly oiled 8 x 8 baking pan and bake in a preheated oven at 425 degrees for about 20 minutes or until golden brown. Cut into 3-inch squares and serve hot.

Serves 8

CALABACITAS

Native Americans have been eating chiles, squash, and corn for thousands of years. This traditional, mildly spiced dish is so easy, and you won't believe the flavor.

½ white onion, chopped fine

1 clove garlic, minced

2 tablespoons corn oil

1 Roma tomato, chopped fine

1 serrano chile, chopped fine

¼ cup frozen corn, thawed

4 medium Mexican gray or zucchini squash
   (about 1 pound), chopped into ½-inch
   cubes

Salt to taste

Pinch of Mexican oregano

2 tablespoons queso cotija or grated
   Monterey Jack cheese

Over medium heat, sauté the onion and garlic in corn oil until soft but not browned. Add the tomato and chile; continue frying for about 5 minutes more. Add the corn, zucchini, and salt. Cover and cook for 5 minutes more. Remove lid and continue sautéing, stirring constantly, until excess juice in absorbed. Add the oregano. Serve hot, topped with a little cheese.

Serves 6

LIME-PICKLED RED ONION

This pickled red onion is quick and easy. It's also an amazing side for any grilled fish, poultry, or meat.

1 red onion, sliced very thin

Juice of 4 key limes

2 tablespoons chopped fresh cilantro

1 tablespoon extra virgin olive oil

1 teaspoon salt

1 teaspoon brown sugar

½ teaspoon dried Mexican oregano

Mix all ingredients together in a nonreactive bowl. Cover and let marinate in a cool place for 3 hours. It will keep in the refrigerator for 3 or 4 days.

Makes 1½ cups

COEURS A LA CRÈME (HEARTS OF CREAM)

This is the perfect ending after a night of spicy New Mexican cuisine. It will cool down the palate and it's so yummy. I always tell folks this easy desert is the older, sexier sister of the cheesecake!

¾ pound softened cream cheese

1 cup sour cream

3 tablespoons confectioners' sugar

½ teaspoon pure vanilla extract

½ teaspoon freshly squeezed lemon juice

Pinch of salt

Beat together all ingredients until smooth. Work cream mixture through a fine sieve, removing any lumps. Line Coeurs a la Crème molds with a single sheet of dampened cheesecloth, large enough to fold back over filling. Divide cream mixture between molds. Fold cheesecloth over mixture and lightly press on cloth. Place molds in a pan (to catch any drippings) in the refrigerator for at least 4 hours and up to 2 days. Unmold Coeurs a la Crème and carefully remove cheesecloth. Let stand at room temperature for 20 minutes before serving. Top with Fresh Blackberry Sauce (see below).

Serves 6

FRESH BLACKBERRY SAUCE

This easy sauce is for topping Coeurs a la Crème (see above), but it's also delicious over grilled fruit.

1 pint fresh blackberries

1 teaspoon sugar

½ teaspoon freshly squeezed
   lemon juice

Place half of the berries in a mixing bowl. Add the sugar and mash the berries well. Add remaining berries and the lemon juice. Mix well. Set aside for 30 minutes for flavors to develop.

Makes 2 cups

COWBOYS

ARIZONA HAS THE LEAST-DEFINED CUISINE in the Chile Belt. It was
settled in the late 1800s by Mormon ranchers and farmers, and inhabited by outlaws and cowboys. When not
shooting at the local natives or the folks in Sonora,
Mexico, these early pioneers looked to both for trade.
When thinking of the past, names like Wyatt Earp,
Geronimo, Cochise, and Pancho Villa come to mind. Life
in this rugged western melting pot was just like these
dubious characters—hard and unforgiving. The resulting
cuisine was a sort of farm-, cowboy-, Sonoran-style Mexican
food that borrowed anything it could from the natives.

Around the turn of the last century, doctors would often send patients with breathing problems "out West" to Arizona to breathe the clean desert air and soak in the natural hot springs. There is a little town west of Phoenix called Tonopah, which the locals tell me translates to "hot water under bush." Tap water can be as hot as 125 degrees, so a major problem is cooling down

The prawns in my recipe for Arizona Freshwater Prawn Scampi (page 122) are fat, juicy, and delicious, with a delicate flavor that is much sweeter than prawns and shrimp caught in the ocean.

Another thing that this region can boast about is Tucson, which has the most authentic northern Mexican food in the nation. Arizona was the last region in the Chile Belt

The only real outside influence on Tucson has been Mexico.

the water. The solution is very inventive. The locals buy the biggest water heater they can find, remove the insulation, and leave the unit unplugged. Then above ground, the water cools off (a little) in the tank.

In the desert south of Tonopah, where the groundwater temperatures are closer to 100 degrees, a new industry has evolved. The water is just the right temperature for raising freshwater prawns. Until recently this has been done only in tropical climates.

to become heavily populated. The Tucson Mexican food scene is relatively new—about one hundred years old compared to New Mexico's four hundred years—but since that time the cuisine has not changed. The only real outside influence on Tucson has been Mexico. The food is sort of locked in a Mexican time warp. I've heard this said about the Mexican food of Phoenix, but it simply doesn't hold true. Although Phoenix has some delightful, very authentic Mexican food, it's more hit-and-miss. The Mexican food in Phoenix runs from Tex-Mex to New Mexican, with everything in between. The good news is that we are seeing more and more authentic Mexican restaurants in Phoenix.

Living in Mesa, Arizona, is a world-renowned chili cook by the name of Andy Householder, whom I first met in the early '90s. He wanted me to help him develop a commercial chili powder based on his book *How to Make A Championship Chili and Win!!!* Andy has spent more time thinking about the process of chili competition than anyone I know. He goes so far as to discuss how to get the Styrofoam judging cup to smell like chili before you put the chili in. Although most won't admit it, many world chili cook-off champions have followed his advice and used the recipe in his book. They also buy and use his wonderful "Mr. HOGG'S Championship Chili Blend" on a regular basis!

Arizona is also home to the biggest salsa-making competition in the world. Each spring the Hemophilia Association of Arizona puts on the Tostito's Southwest Salsa Challenge in old-town Scottsdale. The Hemophilia Association's director, Mike Rosenthal, has been quoted as saying, "I'm throwing a little party for 30,000 of my closest friends!" The one-day event brings in around $250,000 for the charity, which, among other things, sends children with hemophilia and related bleeding disorders to a summer camp. In the Valley of the Sun, the Salsa Challenge is the best party of the year. Between 25,000 and 30,000 people show up for a day of fun, sun, live music, and salsa. At last count the 60 contestants made a record 732 gallons of salsa on-site, yielding 187,392 samples. Along with every drop of salsa, the crowd consumed 7,000 Margaritas, 15,000 beers, 10,000 cold nonalcoholic beverages, several tons of corn chips, a few thousand burritos, hamburgers, and hot dogs, and went through 15 tons of ice. Local salsa-making legend Tim Whillhite once again won grand champion with his Salsa Timeteo. For as long as anyone can remember, Tim has either won the grand championship or taken the trophy for first place in an individual category! This guy has forgotten more about using chiles and making salsa than most of us will ever learn!

The current food scene in Arizona makes use of a wide variety of both fresh and dried chiles. But it wasn't always that way. The only fresh chile that was always available in the '50s was the chile güero, with seasonal availability of fresh jalapeños and green chiles out of New Mexico. Güero is a broad category of chile. Varieties called güero run from mild to very hot and vary in size from 1/2 inch around to several inches long. The name means "pale skinned" and is also a Mexican slang term for "gringo." The güero found in Arizona has about the same dimensions and flavor as the jalapeño but has a sharper point and is a little hotter.

The tepin, which grows wild throughout Sonora, Mexico, is another noted chile. Bright red and a little smaller than a pea, it is one of the hottest chiles in the world. I have used them for years and often find them, ounce for ounce, as hot as any habanero, although some dispute this fact. After harvesting by hand, they are sun-dried and sent to market. As a boy working construction around Phoenix, I often saw migrant workers from Mexico keep a few chile tepins in their top shirt pocket to spice up their lunch!

In this chapter we'll take a look at the current trends in "Sonoran" cuisine. I'll also throw in a few of the more colorful recipes from the early years, including a recipe for a delicious spicy glaze for grill-roasted poultry made from the fruit of the prickly pear cactus.

The cuisine of this region is yet to be defined. What I can tell you is, it's more bistro than fine dining—mild to medium spicy, western, definitely Mexican, and still evolving. Over the past few years we've seen several food crazes come and go. Who knows—the next big wave to take America by storm just might be this Sonoran-style cooking!

GRILL-ROASTED PRIME RIB OF BEEF WITH ASSORTED WILD MUSHROOM AND POBLANO CHILE REDUCTION SAUCE

Since the weather is so hot in Arizona, no one wants to heat up the house by baking. So we do this out on the grill.

1 standing rib roast*
Several sprigs fresh rosemary
Paprika
Granulated garlic
Fresh black pepper

Place baking stone on grill, light burners, and turn to low. Allow grill to heat up slowly to about 350 degrees, turn off burners directly below baking stone, and adjust heat to maintain approximately 350 degrees.

Tuck the rosemary in between the bones of the roast. Season the top of the roast with equal parts of the spices. Place in a roasting pan that can also be used on the stovetop later for making the sauce. Cook the roast in the grill until it reaches an internal temperature of 115 degrees to 120 degrees. Remove from the grill and let rest for 30 minutes. This is for medium-rare, which is pink, not red, in the center. Serve with Assorted Wild Mushroom and Poblano Chile Reduction Sauce (see next page).

*Have your butcher cut away the bones and then tie them back on; this adds flavor and aids in the cooking process. Besides, your dog will love the bones.

About 8 ounces of prime rib per serving

ASSORTED WILD MUSHROOM AND POBLANO CHILE REDUCTION SAUCE

After grill-roasting your favorite beef or pork in a pan that can also be used on the stovetop (see previous page), prepare this wonderful sauce with the pan drippings.

2 (½-ounce) bags assorted dried wild mushrooms

2 cups water

2 shallots, minced

2 cloves garlic, minced

½ cup sliced crimini mushrooms

1 tablespoon olive oil

2 tablespoons all-purpose flour

2 tablespoons olive oil

1 cup red wine

2 poblano chiles, roasted, seeded, and skinned

1 level teaspoon chopped fresh thyme

Salt and pepper to taste

In a small saucepan, simmer the dried mushrooms in the water for 20 minutes. Meanwhile, in a frying pan sauté the shallots, garlic, and mushrooms in 1 tablespoon of olive oil until the mushrooms are golden brown. Make a medium-brown roux by frying the flour in 2 tablespoons of olive oil; set aside but keep warm. Deglaze the roasting pan with the red wine and then add the mushrooms along with the simmering liquid. Cook to reduce for about 5 minutes over medium heat (it may be necessary to add a little more water). Add mushrooms and chiles. If sauce is too thin, stir in a little of the roux to desired consistency. Stir in thyme, season with salt and pepper, and serve.

Makes about 3½ cups

Sri Lanka's *Daily News* reported that a would-be rapist, age 62, was foiled when his intended victim, age 56, threw a bottle of chile sauce on his naked body. The man "remained several hours under water in great pain" before he was arrested.

E-ROASTED TRI-TIP OF BEEF
H JOE'S WORLD-FAMOUS MEXICAN BEER MARINADE

*the past several years I have cooked the Annual Road Rally Dinner at the So-Cal Speed Shop in
oenix. We set up in the parking lot and serve more than six hundred people while they're looking at
ome of the most beautiful vintage cars you've ever seen. For the main course I always make this
easily prepared tri-tip roast, served on fresh handmade rolls. The #1 comment I get is, "That's the
best piece of meat I've ever eaten!" Try it. You won't be sorry.*

1 (3-pound) tri-tip roast

Marinade:

¾ cup soy sauce

½ cup dark Mexican beer

⅓ cup olive oil

3 tablespoons white vinegar

½ white onion, diced

1 tablespoon crushed red chile

1 tablespoon Italian seasoning

3 cloves garlic, minced

1 teaspoon dark brown sugar

1 teaspoon freshly ground black pepper

Whisk all ingredients together in a nonreactive bowl. Add tri-tip roast
and marinate overnight, turning every couple of hours. Grill roast until a
digital thermometer reaches 128 degrees when inserted at the thickest
part of the tri-tip. Remove from heat and allow to rest for 10 minutes
before slicing across the grain. It's even better cold the next day; but
when it tastes this good, leftovers are hard to come by.

Serves 6 to 8

**Archaeologists in Mexico have discovered evidence that during prehistoric times
as far back as 7500 BC, natives were eating wild chiles related to the chiltepin.**

SPICY GRILL-ROASTED PORK ROULADE WITH HERBED CALIMYRNA FIGS AND ARIZONA SWEET ONION

Forget Maui or Walla Walla. Arizona grows the best sweet onions in the country.

Filling:

6 dried Calimyrna figs, minced

2 Arizona sweet onions, chopped fine

Zest of 2 lemons

1 poblano chile, roasted, peeled, and
   chopped

⅓ cup finely chopped Italian parsley

4 cloves garlic, minced

2 tablespoons finely chopped rosemary

2 tablespoons marjoram

2 tablespoons brown sugar

Freshly ground black pepper to taste

1 (4-pound) boneless pork loin, butterflied

2 sprigs fresh rosemary

2 teaspoons extra virgin olive oil

1 cup medium-bodied red wine

1½ cups beef or pork stock

4 tablespoons sweet butter, cut into small
   pieces

Combine all filling ingredients. Lay pork roast on flat surface, cut side up, and spread filling evenly over top. Roll roast up and tie closed with butcher's twine. Brown roast on grill. Remove from grill and stuff rosemary sprigs under twine. Indirectly grill-bake the roast in a baking pan until roast reaches an internal temperature of 138 degrees. Remove from baking pan and set on platter, allowing roast to rest for 30 minutes before slicing.

Meanwhile, mix the olive oil, wine, stock, and pan drippings together and bring to a simmer. Reduce by a third, remove from heat, and swirl in butter. Serve over slices of roulade.

Serves 12

SPICY GRILL-ROASTED CHICKEN WITH APRICOT, PECAN, AND POBLANO CHILE GLAZE

Do you love chicken, but need a new way to prepare it? This easy recipe is a delicious Sonoran twist on grilled chicken. It's one of those dishes that receives high marks on every level. It smells great while it's grill-roasting and looks beautiful at the table, and the flavor is out of this world! (You can also make this in the oven.)

1 whole roasting chicken

¼ cup apricot jelly or preserves

¼ cup red pepper jelly

¼ cup water

¼ cup whole pecans

1 Poblano chile, roasted and peeled, seeds and stem removed and then chopped fine

Salt and pepper to taste

With a sharp knife, cut through the breastbone of the chicken, lengthwise (your butcher can do this for you). Open the chicken up and turn it over. Press down on the back until it cracks, causing the bird to lay flat. Grill-roast the chicken over hot coals or in a hot gas grill until it starts to brown. Put the bird in a spot on the grill, without direct heat below. (This is known as indirect grilling it reduces the chance of a flare up.) Close the lid on the grill. Grilling the chicken should take about 1 hour, depending on your grill. The chicken is done when a digital thermometer inserted in the thickest part of the breast and thigh reads 165 degrees F.

Meanwhile, make the glaze by whisking together the two jellies and water in a small saucepan and bringing to a boil. Add the pecans and chopped poblano chile; stir together and let cool. Spoon over the chicken in the last 10 minutes of indirect grilling, as the sugar will burn if it roasts too long. Season to taste with the salt and pepper, and serve.

Serves 6

"The chile, it seems to me, is one of the few foods that has its own god."
Diana Kennedy, Mexican cookbook author

POLLO ASADO TROPICAL

This is my variation on the mesquite-smoked chicken served at Mexican parillas or grills in the Phoenix area. They use a similar seasoning and yellow food coloring. I've substituted turmeric for the food coloring, which adds an extra depth of flavor naturally. This recipe works well when the chicken is indirectly grilled, smoked, or baked.

2 whole split chickens

Marinade:

½ gallon orange juice

1 white onion, chopped

4 or 5 cloves garlic, minced

2 tablespoons extra virgin olive oil

¼ cup ground turmeric

¼ cup Latin seasoning salt*

2 tablespoons brown sugar

1 (20-ounce) can pineapple rings in their
   own juice

4 dried chile de arbol, or 2 teaspoons
   crushed red chile

Whisk together the orange juice, onion, garlic, olive oil, turmeric, seasoning salt, and brown sugar in a deep mixing bowl or large nonreactive container. Stir in the pineapple and its juice along with the dried chiles. Place the chicken in the marinade, submerging and turning to coat well, and cover with plastic wrap. Keep refrigerated overnight, turning every 6 hours.

Remove the chicken and pineapple from the marinade; indirectly grill, smoke, or oven-bake until it reaches an internal temperature of 165 degrees at the center of the breast. Discard the marinade; there's no need to use it for basting because the chicken is so juicy!

*The Latino markets in the Southwest sell a product at the butcher counters called *adobo*. It's a type of seasoning salt. It will say on the bottle whether it is for meat, chicken, or pork. Make sure you get the one that includes chicken. It is made by several different companies. I use Chef Merito brand, but I think they are all about the same. In a pinch you can substitute generic reddish seasoning salt. Enjoy!

Serves 8 to 10 hungry people

PRICKLY PEAR SYRUP

My home in Cave Creek is at the northern end of the Sonoran Desert, which is thick and lush with mesquite, ironwood, and palo verde. There are many varieties of cactus—the saguaro, staghorn, barrel, and cholla, to name a few. This region is also home to the prickly pear (Opuntia engelmannii and Opuntia phaeacantha). The blood-red fruit of the prickly pear is called tuna. *This cactus is so prevalent in my neighborhood that every August it's like living in a tuna orchard. We use the syrup to top desserts and warm, toasted bread, to glaze poultry, and to enhance our Margaritas. My wife, Chef Kathy, makes up a batch of prickly pear wine every few years with our good friend and neighbor Ed Fedoruk. The Native Americans living in the Southwest have used tunas for food and for dyeing cloth. While preparing the syrup, wear rubber gloves and an apron to prevent staining. Ask your grocer for tunas or commercially made prickly pear syrup.*

24 prickly pears
½ cup mesquite blossom honey
2 teaspoons freshly squeezed lemon juice

Use tongs to wash fruit. Allow fruit to dry and then roughly chop into smaller pieces; don't worry about removing the skin or stickers. Run the fruit through a blender or food processor until pureed very well. Work the puree through a fine sieve with a rubber spatula; discard the solids. In a small saucepan over medium heat, bring the prickly pear juice, honey, and lemon juice to a boil; reduce heat and simmer for 10 minutes. Remove from heat and allow to cool. For convenience, pour syrup into a plastic squeeze bottle while it's still warm. Syrup may be stored in the refrigerator for up to 12 days.

Makes 2 cups

"Chili is not so much food as a state of mind. Addictions to it are formed early in life and the victims never recover. On blue days in October, I get this passionate yearning for a bowl of chili, and I nearly lose my mind." Margaret Cousins, novelist

ROASTED CORNISH GAME HENS WITH RUBY PRICKLY PEAR AND RED CHILE GLAZE

Not only is this glaze delicious, but the ruby color is outstanding at the table. Use it on Cornish game hens as well as other types of poultry. Prickly pear syrup is now available through your grocer if you don't want to make it from scratch.

2 fresh Cornish game hens

½ cup red chile jelly

2 tablespoons Prickly Pear Syrup (page 120)

Thin the red chile jelly with Prickly Pear Syrup. Roast game hens to an internal temperature of 155 degrees. Baste with glaze and continue roasting until they reach an internal temperature of 165 degrees. Keep your eye on these; they have a tendency to burn, due to the sugar.

Serves 4

GRILLED SONORAN SEA BASS

The Sea of Cortez is only four hours away from Phoenix. Its fish and seafood is among the best in the world. This tropical marinade is wonderful with any medium-firm light-flavored fish.

4 sea bass steaks

Marinade:

½ cup freshly squeezed orange juice

¼ cup safflower oil

3 tablespoons lime juice

1 tablespoon tequila

3 serrano chiles, minced fine

1 teaspoon dark brown sugar

½ teaspoon paprika

Pinch allspice

Zest of 1 lime

1 clove garlic, minced

Whisk all ingredients for marinade together in a large nonreactive bowl. Marinate fish for 3 hours, turning often. Grill over mesquite charcoal until fish is done (about 10 minutes per inch of thickness).

Serves 4

ARIZONA FRESHWATER PRAWN SCAMPI

Shrimp raised in the desert—hmmm, sounds like one of those famous Arizona land deals. The truth is, due to the geothermal wells in the desert below Buckeye, all the conditions are right for raising freshwater shrimp, which are much sweeter than those from the ocean, and in this dish they're scrumptious.

24 large freshwater prawns, unpeeled

1 lemon

½ cup extra virgin olive oil

8 cloves garlic, minced

1 teaspoon crushed red pepper

¼ teaspoon dried basil

¼ teaspoon dried chervil

¼ teaspoon dried ground thyme

Salt and freshly ground black pepper to
    taste

1 cup dry white wine

2 tablespoons butter

2 tablespoons Italian parsley, chopped fine

Rinse the prawns well. Using a sharp knife, slice through the shell of the prawns along the back but do not cut in half. Squeeze the lemon over the prawns and rub the juice in.

Heat the oil in a large sauté pan over medium heat. Add the shrimp, turn up the heat a little, and sauté for 3 to 4 minutes until the prawns are pink. Add garlic, red pepper, spices, salt, and pepper. Stir well. Remove prawns to serving plate.

Deglaze pan with white wine. Reduce wine sauce by half over high heat (about 1 minute). Remove from heat and stir in butter. Spoon wine sauce over prawns and garnish with parsley.

Serves 4

 The Spanish term *habanero* **means "from Havana."**

CHILLED AVOCADO SOUP WITH SONORAN SHRIMP CONFETTI

I worked on a morning television show in Phoenix with mostly female viewers for four years. I came up with this recipe after I was asked to do something that was both Sonoran and elegant. This is light and fresh summertime eating at its best!

Soup:

4 ripe avocados, peeled, seeded, and
    chopped
2 cups half-and-half
2 cups sour cream
1 cup fat-free chicken broth
5 green onions, chopped fine
2 cloves garlic, chopped fine
1 large shallot, chopped fine
1 serrano chile, chopped fine
Juice of 4 key limes
½ teaspoon green habanero sauce, or
    Tabasco Habanero Sauce, or Louisiana
    hot sauce
Dash of Worcestershire sauce
Salt and white pepper to taste

Sonoran Shrimp Confetti:

1 red bell pepper, cut into matchstick-size
    pieces
¾ cup matchstick-size pieces of jicama
2 poblano chiles, roasted, peeled, and
    chopped
¾ pound cooked shrimp, cut into bite-size
    chunks and chilled
½ bunch cilantro, chopped
Salt and black pepper to taste

Working in batches, run the soup ingredients through a food processor until smooth and creamy. Stir together well in a large glass bowl or terrine. Cover with plastic wrap and place in the refrigerator to chill.

Meanwhile, toss the confetti ingredients together in a separate bowl, cover with plastic wrap, and place in the refrigerator to chill. Once both the soup and confetti are fully chilled, ladle the soup into cold soup bowls and place a big scoop of the confetti in the center of each bowl. Serve with a crisp, cold white wine.

Serves 6

CHIPOTLE CILANTRO FETTUCCINI

With the convergence of cultures in Arizona, we are constantly seeing wonderful new dishes like this. Latin meets Latinos!

1 can chipotle chiles, drained and chopped fine (reserve adobo sauce)

¼ cup cilantro, chopped fine

1 clove garlic, chopped fine

2 cups bread flour

1 tablespoon adobo sauce (from canned chipotles)

2 large eggs

1 teaspoon salt

2 teaspoons extra virgin olive oil

Using a dough blade, combine the chiles, cilantro, and garlic with flour, adobo sauce, eggs, and salt. While machine is running, drizzle in the oil. Dough will come together as a crumbly mixture. Add 1 tablespoon of water at a time until dough forms a ball. Remove dough from food processor. If dough sticks to your hands, work a little flour into the mixture.

Roll dough into a ball and cut into quarters. Flatten one of the quarters with the palm of your hand. Run the dough through the pasta machine four times on the #1 (or largest) setting, each time folding the dough into thirds. If dough is sticky, dust with flour during this process. Run the pasta through the #2 setting and then the #3, #4, and #5 settings. Now, move the handle to the fettuccini blade, dust the pasta with flour, and run it through. At this point, it may be necessary to pull a few strands of the pasta apart, depending on the texture of the dough.

Drop the pasta into boiling water for 30 to 45 seconds or to desired texture. Garnish pasta with whatever toppings you like. Suggestion: try olive oil, chives, and a good Romano cheese.

Serves 4

CHIPOTLE AND CHEDDAR MASHED POTATOES WITH ROASTED GARLIC

Everybody likes mashed potatoes. The addition of smoky chipotles, white cheddar, and roasted garlic makes this fantastic side something to write home about. Next morning, make potato patties with eggs for breakfast. Just the aroma of these delicious potatoes will drive your family crazy.

1 bulb of garlic

2½ pounds white potatoes, peeled and cut into cubes

2 canned chipotle chiles

1 tablespoon adobo sauce (from canned chipotles)

1½ cups grated white cheddar cheese

½ cup cream

2 tablespoons sweet butter

Salt and freshly ground black pepper to taste

Cut off the pointed end off the garlic bulb exposing the end of the individual cloves. Wrap the bulb in foil and place in a 350-degree oven for 25 to 30 minutes or until garlic is lightly browned and soft. Allow the garlic to cool enough to handle and then squeeze out the roasted garlic paste.

Meanwhile, boil the potatoes in a large pot of salted water for 20 minutes or until tender; remove from heat but leave potatoes in the hot water.

Mash the chipotle chiles along with the adobo sauce and set aside.

Remove the potatoes from the hot water and mash well along with 2 tablespoons of the roasted garlic paste. Immediately mash in the chipotles, cheese, cream, and butter until creamy and the cheese is fully melted. Season to taste; cover until serving.

Serves 6

Washing your hands with a mild bleach solution will help remove the burning sensation caused by handling chiles.

SONORAN BLACK BEAN AND JICAMA SALAD

What the heck is a jicama? Well, it's that sort of lumpy, potatoish, spaceship-looking thing in the produce section (ask the produce guy). Anyway, it tastes like a cross between a potato and an apple.

¼ cup freshly squeezed key lime juice

¼ cup extra virgin olive oil

1 tablespoon Dijon mustard

3 cups black beans, cooked

½ red bell pepper, roasted, peeled, and chopped

½ yellow bell pepper, roasted, peeled, and chopped

½ poblano chile, roasted, peeled, and chopped

1½ cups chopped Roma tomatoes

¾ cup julienned jicama, 2 inches long

½ cup chopped celery

¾ cup chopped cilantro

¼ cup minced red onion

¼ cup chopped Italian parsley

1 jalapeño chile, seeded and minced

½ teaspoon ground cumin

½ teaspoon salt

½ teaspoon freshly ground black pepper

Whisk together the lime juice, oil, and mustard. Warm in a saucepan along with the beans, bell peppers, and poblano chiles for 5 minutes or until beans are fully warmed. Remove from heat, stir in all other ingredients, and serve.

Serves 6

The Mayas hurled chiles at their enemies with a catapult in an effort to blind and stun!

SONORAN B.L.T. SALAD

This is a local twist on the Italian favorite, Panzanella. It's a great summertime salad. When we take it to a barbecue we just call it B.L.T. Salad. If we serve it at dinner . . . well, that's a different matter. It's then called Sonoran Panzanella.

Salad:

4 cups assorted small tomatoes (cherry, grape, yellow pear, etc.)

2 tablespoons canola oil

4 cups good crusty French or Italian bread, cut into ¾-inch cubes and dried overnight

6 slices thick-cut hardwood-smoked bacon, chopped and then fried, drippings reserved

1 poblano chile, roasted, skinned, and chopped

½ avocado, peeled, seeded, and chopped

1 cup watercress leaves, rinsed well

2 cups chopped romaine lettuce

Dressing:

¼ cup balsamic vinegar

1 teaspoon salt

1 teaspoon black pepper

2 tablespoons chiffonade* of basil leaves

1 tablespoon chiffonade* of mint leaves

3 tablespoons extra virgin olive oil

Freshly grated Parmesan cheese for topping

Cut the tomatoes into very small pieces. (I cut the cherry tomatoes in quarters and the smaller tomatoes in half.) In a hot pan, fry half of the tomatoes in the canola oil until they start to brown and dry out a little, remove from pan, and set aside to cool.

In a large serving bowl, toss the dried bread in the bacon drippings. In a separate bowl, whisk together all dressing ingredients except the oil. Then drizzle in the oil while whisking to emulsify. Add all other salad ingredients, including the fried tomatoes, to the bread and toss well. Drizzle in the dressing and toss again. Serve on chilled plates, topped with a little freshly grated Parmesan cheese, and with a good, cold, crisp Sauvignon Blanc or Pinot Gris.

*Chiffonade is a French cooking term for laying leaves on top of one another, rolling them up like a cigarette, and then cutting them very fine the short way. Heck, you've probably been chiffonading for years and didn't even know it!

Serves 6 to 8

BUTTERMILK TEQUILA SALAD DRESSING

This easy salad dressing is a classic example of Arizona fine dining meets old Mexico.

6 tablespoons buttermilk

2 tablespoons mayonnaise

½ cup crème fraiche or sour cream

¼ cup plain yogurt

2 tablespoons tequila reposado

1 roasted poblano chile, seeds and veins
   removed, chopped very fine

2 cloves garlic, minced

½ tablespoon finely chopped Italian parsley

2 teaspoons key lime juice

½ teaspoon salt

½ teaspoon white pepper

½ teaspoon brown sugar

Whisk together the buttermilk, mayonnaise, crème fraiche, yogurt, and tequila. Stir in all other ingredients. Set aside in the refrigerator for 1 hour for flavors to marry.

Makes 2 cups

SWEET CHILE PECANS

These are an easy snack. Folks eat them like candy, and they are out of this world as a substitute for croutons.

¼ cup sugar, divided

½ teaspoon salt

1 teaspoon paprika

2 teaspoons canola oil (or any neutral-fla-
   vored oil)

1 cup whole pecans

In a mixing bowl, combine half the sugar with the salt and paprika; mix well. Heat the oil in a large, heavy frying pan. Lightly brown the nuts, stirring constantly until they release their fragrance, about 2 minutes (be careful; they will burn very quickly). Sprinkle in the remaining sugar, shaking the pan constantly to keep the nuts from burning. When the sugar melts and caramelizes, stir well and remove from heat. Immediately toss the nuts in the sugar-spice mixture, separating them with two forks to avoid burning your fingers (if the sugar cools down, it will set). Once the nuts have cooled, they will keep for 2 weeks in an airtight container.

Makes 1 cup

SONORAN FRUIT KABOBS

There is a dish served on hot days in Sonora, Mexico, called pico de gallo. It is a fruit salad that also contains cucumber and jicama. The following recipe is the same soothing fruit salad on skewers. The refreshing addition of lime and chile will amaze you!

1 pineapple

1 pint (2 cups) large strawberries

4 cups assorted ripe melons, peeled and cut into 1-inch cubes

½ jicama, peeled and cut into 1-inch cubes

½ cucumber, peeled and cut into 1-inch cubes

Juice of 4 key limes

Cayenne pepper or paprika

Cut the top 3 inches off the pineapple and set aside. Cut the bottom and skin off the pineapple and discard. The center of the pineapple is hard so cut around it, removing large pieces of pineapple. Cut those pieces into 1-inch chunks.

Thread the skewers with each of the following, alternating colors: pineapple, strawberry, one piece of each melon, jicama, and cucumber. Follow the same pattern with each skewer. Squeeze lime juice over each skewer and then sprinkle with cayenne or paprika.

Set the top of the pineapple in the center of a large plate. Starting down low and working from side to side, poke the skewers into the pineapple. Spread the skewers out evenly for a beautiful edible centerpiece.

Makes about 20 skewers

SONORAN MILKSHAKE

Tired of Margaritas but want tequila? This is an elegant after-dinner drink.

1½ ounces Chambord liqueur

1½ ounces of your favorite tequila blanco

2 ounces half-and-half

Shake and serve on ice in an old-fashioned glass.

Makes 1 cocktail

MOJITOS

People often think the favored cocktail around Arizona is the Margarita. Sure we drink margaritas, but when people come to a party at my house we make Mojitos. We start out with a 4-gallon glass crock, 1/2 gallon of light rum, 60 key limes, and mix to taste from there.

Ice

6 ounces light rum

12 mint or spearmint sprigs, 8 roughly
    broken apart

6 tablespoons fresh lime juice

4 tablespoons sugar

Club soda

4 slices lime

Place ice in beverage shaker; add rum, the 8 broken-up mint sprigs, lime juice, and sugar. Shake well and serve over ice in a highball glass. Top off each glass with a splash of club soda and garnish with a slice of lime and a sprig of mint.

Makes 4 cocktails

CALIFORNIANS

TAKING THE LONG DRIVE WEST OUT OF PHOENIX on I-10 always
seems slow and hot, even in the cooler months. I can't
help but remember this same drive as a boy with my family.
No air-conditioning in those days—just hot, sticky vinyl
seats. Seven of us in all, packed into our 1962 dark blue
Ford station wagon. When we would get restless, my dad
would reminisce about traveling with his family when he
was a boy during the Great Depression. Back then the only
road went through the sand dunes by Yuma. He remembered helping his father break off pieces of the old wooden
plank road to build a fire so my grandma could cook supper.

California cuisine is probably the most difficult cuisine in the Chile Belt to define. California, like New Mexico, was settled by Catholic missionaries, and like the foods of New Mexico, the original California cuisine was basically a cross between European/Spanish influence and native peoples of the region. The difference, though, is that once the California Gold Rush opened the door, people just kept on coming: gold prospectors, railroad workers, farmers, ranchers, the film industry, and immigrants from around the world. Later, in the 1950s, people looking for the good life swarmed to the coast. In the 1960s came the surfers, the vegetarians, and the hippies. In the 1970s California saw the explosion of Silicon Valley. With the influence of every new invasion, the culinary scene constantly changes and redefines itself. Combine that with four distinct influences: First, the large-scale cultivation of a staggering variety of fruits and vegetables (including chiles), made possible by the state's warm climate, rich soil, and abundant water. Second, the availability of some of the best seafood in the world. Third, the huge number of Mexican emigrants that have poured into California for the past 150 years. And finally, the rich-and-famous in Los Angeles and Hollywood, who have

This is probably the most difficult cuisine in the Chile Belt to define.

enabled California to be on the cutting edge of fashion and food trends for the past 75 years.

The resulting food is Pacific Rim meets Mexican at Hollywood and Vine, while wearing a Grateful Dead T-shirt. Dishes like Soy and Wasabi-Basted Spiny-Lobster Tacos with Crunchy Pear and Avocado Salsa are commonplace. Even the people of California can't come up with a simple description for this ever-evolving culinary phenomenon. So, I think of the food of this region as very fresh and mildly spicy to very hot Pacific Rim fusion cuisine with a Latino flare.

One of the driving forces behind the ongoing development of food trends in California is the availability of the freshest produce from all over the world. This availability can be attributed partly to the world-famous City Market of Los Angeles. Over the years as I've developed new recipes and looked for some obscure produce item, especially chiles, my contacts at several different sources have told me, "I'll check with the L.A. Market." It's *the* place to go for the best produce in this part of the world!

Years ago many varieties of chiles were unknown or just not available. Due to sources like the Market, they are now just a phone call away, if not already at your local grocer. Back in the 1980s we started hearing about the habanero (translated as "from Havana"), the hottest chile in the world, reported to be as much as fifty times hotter than a jalapeño. Colors include any combination of yellow, orange, red, and green. They were shipped into Phoenix from California, bright orange, pointed, and roughly the size of Ping-Pong balls. In 1990 I attended a lecture on habaneros by Dave DeWitt. He showed a photo of a habanero the size of a bell pepper in the palm of his wife Mary Jane's hand. The flavor of a habanero is unmistakable—a cross between carrot and fruit. We eat them whole, roasted, and drizzled with lime juice and salt.

Old West historian and author Bob "Boze" Bell tells of a night of tequila-drinking and habanero-eating at my house. He says that forty-five minutes after eating the whole chiles: "The pores on the back of my neck were open wide enough to throw quarters in! . . . like my mouth was riding a rocket sled to hell!"

Another chile that we have to order through the L.A. Market is the chile *manzano* (meaning "apple"). Although many northern Mexican recipes suggest substituting serrano or jalapeño, neither have the heat or depth of flavor. It is one of the few chiles used exclusively fresh, never dried. It is found either bright yellow or bright red, each containing dark black seeds. The red variety is much hotter and the yellow has more depth of flavor. It looks like a pointed bell pepper with very smooth skin. Heat level 7–8.

As I think of the California chile scene, a poor Vietnamese emigrant named Huy Fong comes to mind. (I have heard the following story several times; if it's not true it should be!) Upon arriving in California he decided to go into the hot-sauce business, relying on age-old Asian recipes. When it came time to bottle his first batch of hot sauce, he went looking for packaging and found a smoking deal on lime-green bottle caps. They were ugly but money was tight.

Later, after the business picked up, he could afford a more suitable color cap for his Sriracha and Sambal hot sauces. As planned, he switched to a white bottle cap, but sales dropped. Apparently people had no idea of the product's name; they just remembered the lime-green cap and Asian writing on that bottle of delicious hot sauce. So Huy switched back and the rest is another California success story—his hot sauces now ship all over the world.

In this chapter you'll find recipes as diverse as California itself. Wine, goat cheese, fish sauce, pheasant, papaya—all are mixed with a wide variety of chiles. Like California, this chapter is an adventure and a chance to try something new. So make up a shopping list, invite a few good friends over, light the grill, and pop open a good, cold, crisp California chardonnay. As they say in California, you're in for a slice of the good life!

GRILL-ROASTED LOIN OF PORK STUFFED WITH HERBED PEACHES AND POBLANO CHILES

If you only try one recipe in this book, try this. People tell me it's the best thing they have ever eaten in their entire lives. I agree!

Whole loin of pork roast (six bones), with a ¼-inch fat cap (ask your butcher)

2 sticks sweet butter, room temperature

1 bunch fresh thyme

Kosher salt

Freshly ground black pepper

4 poblano chiles, roasted, peeled and chopped

8 fresh peaches, or 2 (16-ounce) cans in natural juices, halved and pitted

Root vegetables: celery root, potatoes, carrots, and/or parsnips

Have the butcher chine the roast, which cuts through the backbone of the roast and allows it to be sliced after cooking. Also have the butcher cut a cavity between the ribs and the loin, leaving the roast connected. Barely score the skin of the roast into the meat in lines running the same direction as the ribs, about 1/2 inch apart.

Mix together the butter, thyme, salt, and pepper. Rub the inside cavity of the roast and then the exterior. Stuff the cavity with chiles and peaches and then tie the roast closed with butcher's string in three or four places. Place the roast in a large baking pan and add any leftover peaches and the root vegetables. In a hot grill, smoker, or oven, roast the pork at 425 degrees for about 1 hour or until the center of the loin reaches an internal temperature of 160 degrees. Remove the roast and allow to rest for 10 minutes before serving.

Serves 6

Famous movie actor Clark Gable's last meal reportedly was a bowl of chili from Chasen's, delivered to him in the hospital the night he died!

PORK, PEPPERS, AND PINEAPPLE SKEWERS WITH SONORAN PONZU

For those hot summer days when you don't want to heat up your kitchen or spend an hour over a flaming grill, you can make these in advance. Toss them on the grill and they're done in 20 minutes!

1 medium pineapple, fresh (it's ripe if fragrant)

2 pounds pork shoulder, cut into 1½-inch pieces

20 assorted peppers (jalapeño, red Fresno, guerro, habanero, to name a few)

Nonstick vegetable oil spray

If using wooden or bamboo skewers, make sure to soak them in water for 30 minutes prior to use so they don't burn on the grill. Cut the top and bottom off the pineapple. Cut the pineapple into quarters from top to bottom, and remove the hard core. Cut remaining slices into 1- to 2-inch chunks.

Thread alternating pieces of pork, pineapple, and peppers onto skewers. Sprinkle well with Sonoran Ponzu Dust (recipe below) and then spray well with nonstick vegetable oil spray. Brown over hot grill or coals; then move skewers away from direct heat and close the lid. Cook for another 20 minutes or until done. Be sure to use a glove or oven mitt when turning or handling skewers, as they will heat up when the lid is closed! Remove from grill and serve with Sonoran Ponzu Sauce (recipe below) in small bowls for dipping. This dish is delicious with grill-baked yams.

Sonoran Ponzu Dust:

½ cup mild New Mexico red chile powder

½ cup brown sugar

¼ cup kosher salt

¼ cup black pepper

Mix together and sprinkle over pork or poultry before grilling.

Sonoran Ponzu Sauce:

1 cup mirin

¾ cup premium Japanese soy sauce

Juice of 2 key limes

1 teaspoon Ground chipotle pepper

Bring the mirin to a simmer. Simmer for 6 to 8 minutes, or until mirin reduces to 1/3 cup. Remove from heat and whisk in all other ingredients. Drizzle over grilled pork, poultry, or seafood, or serve on the side as a dipping sauce.

Serves 6 to 8

SPICY ASIAN COCKTAIL RIBS

This appetizer is pure Pacific Rim—wasabi, sambal, and rice vinegar against roasted pork with soy sauce. These ribs are spicy and delicious.

Marinade:

¼ cup seasoned rice wine vinegar

1½ tablespoons wasabi powder

2 tablespoons unsulfered molasses

⅔ cup pure maple syrup

½ cup Dijon mustard

½ cup sambal

2 tablespoons soy sauce

3 to 4 pounds baby back ribs (have your butcher cut them in half lengthwise, and then cut into individual ribs)

Kosher salt and freshly ground black pepper to taste

Preheat oven to 375 degrees. Mix rice wine vinegar and wasabi together until smooth; add remaining ingredients and mix together well. Pour mixture over the ribs, cover, and marinate them for 1 hour covered in the refrigerator.

Place ribs on a cookie sheet or shallow baking pan. Season the ribs with salt and pepper and bake for about 30 minutes, basting twice. Turn ribs and baste again. Roast for 15 minutes more or until fully cooked and glazed. Do not baste during the last 15 minutes. Discard unused marinade. Serve warm.

Serves 10

FRUITED SAUVIGNON BLANC GLAZE

This is a good place to see how diverse chile flavors can be. I made his recipe for pheasant but it works well with any poultry or roast pork!

1 cup sauvignon blanc wine

½ cup chopped dried apricots

2 tablespoons dried cherries or assorted berries

Bring the wine to a boil in a small saucepan over high heat. Stir in the dried fruit and remove from heat. Let stand for 30 minutes before basting Grill-Roasted Pheasant (page 143).

Makes about 1 cup

GRILL-ROASTED PHEASANT WITH MANZANO CHILE AND FRUITED SAUVIGNON BLANC GLAZE

This recipe screams California. On my TV show we always called pheasant "Date Chicken." You know, you have date clothes and date music . . .the slow, romantic stuff. Well, this dish is what roast chicken wishes it was. No grill? No problem. You can also prepare this in a 350-degree oven.

1 (2½-pound) pheasant

1 orange, cut in half

3 cloves garlic

1 shallot, chopped

4 sprigs Italian parsley, roughly chopped

4 tablespoons sweet butter, softened

3 slices hardwood-smoked bacon

Fruited Sauvignon Blanc Glaze (page 142)

½ manzano chile, seeds and veins removed, shredded (wear rubber gloves)

Place pizza stone on grill. Light burners and turn to low. Allow grill to slowly heat up to about 350 degrees; then turn burners directly below pizza stone to low and adjust heat to maintain approximately 350 degrees.

Rub the inside cavity and exterior of the pheasant with the juice of half of the orange. Cut remaining orange half into three chunks. Place orange chunks, garlic, shallot, and parsley into the cavity of the pheasant. Spread the butter over the pheasant breast and then lay the bacon crosswise over the breast. Put the pheasant in a baking dish and cover with a lid or foil. Grill-bake for 45 minutes.

While the pheasant roasts, make the Fruited Sauvignon Blanc Glaze. When pheasant is ready, remove lid or foil and pour the glaze over the bird. Grill-bake for 45 minutes more, basting often with the glaze. When it reaches an internal temperature of 165 degrees at the center of the thigh and breast, sprinkle the chili shreds over the pheasant and baste one more time.

Place the pheasant on a serving plate. Spoon a little more of the glaze over the top of the pheasant and serve with remaining glaze on the side.

Serves 2

GRILLED COCONUT CHICKEN WITH SPICY THAI GLAZE

If you're tired of those same old chicken recipes, try this easy, sweet, and mildly spicy grilled coconut chicken. The enzymes in the coconut milk tenderize the chicken, which produces a delicious grill-roasted chicken that is both tender and very moist.

1 whole chicken

Marinade:

2 (13½-ounce) cans coconut milk

6 ¼-inch slices of fresh ginger, about the size of a quarter

4 (2-inch) pieces lemongrass

1 tablespoon kosher salt

2 teaspoons white pepper

Spicy Thai Glaze:

4 medium Thai chiles, chopped fine (or substitute serranos)

2 tablespoons packed brown sugar

1 cup honey

2 tablespoons soy sauce

1 tablespoon grated fresh ginger

2 teaspoons rice vinegar

Garnish:

2 tablespoons flaked coconut

¼ bunch fresh cilantro, chopped

2 whole scallions, chopped

1 tablespoon white sesame seeds

Wash the chicken under cold water. Cut lengthwise through breast and breastbone, turn chicken over and press down on back while spreading the breast until the back cracks and chicken lays flat. In a large glass baking dish, whisk the coconut milk until the solids are well incorporated. Toss in the ginger, lemongrass, salt, and pepper, and stir well. Place the chicken in the marinade, skin side down. Turn the chicken over and spoon marinade on any parts that did not get fully coated. Marinate overnight in the refrigerator, turning 2 or 3 times.

Indirectly (not directly over the flame) grill-roast the chicken until it reaches an internal temperature of 165 degrees.

Meanwhile, bring all the glaze ingredients to a low boil for 2 minutes and set aside. Warm it again when the chicken comes off the grill. Mix all the garnish ingredients together.

Once the chicken is fully cooked, remove from grill to a serving platter. Spoon 1/3 of the warm glaze over the chicken; place remaining glaze in a small bowl to spoon over the chicken servings at the table. Sprinkle glazed chicken liberally with coconut-cilantro garnish and serve immediately.

Serves 6 to 8

TROPICAL FRUITED, SOY-GLAZED SALMON FILLET WITH HABANERO

Frozen fruit juice combinations are sold in the freezer section of your grocery store. This recipe works well with any of them, but the apple-mango-passion fruit juice takes this recipe over the top.

1 (2-pound) salmon fillet, skinned, pin bones removed, and cut into 6 to 8 individual steaks

2 teaspoons white pepper

Vegetable oil spray

¼ cup frozen apple-mango-passion fruit juice concentrate, thawed

¼ cup coarse-grain Dijon mustard

1 tablespoon soy sauce

2 teaspoons Tabasco Habanero sauce (add more for extreme heat)

1 fresh lemon

1 small bunch fresh dill, chopped

Light the grill. Quickly rinse the salmon steaks under cold water and pat dry with a paper towel. Sprinkle both sides with white pepper. Spray both sides with vegetable oil spray. In a small mixing bowl, stir together the fruit juice concentrate, mustard, soy sauce, and habanero sauce.

Turn grill to medium. Place the salmon steaks on the hot grill, skin side up. To keep them from sticking, gently lift the steaks from the grill surface after 10 to 15 seconds and set them back down again. After 2 minutes, gently turn the steaks and once again gently lift them to prevent sticking. Spoon the glaze over the fish, reserving some for the other side. Cook the fish for about 8 minutes more. (The rule for grilling fish is about 10 minutes of grilling for each inch of thickness.) Turn the fish one more time, spoon on the remaining glaze, let cook for 30 seconds, and remove steaks from the grill to a plate. Drizzle with a little lemon juice and top with fresh dill.

Serves 6 to 8

SPICY PACIFIC RIM GRILLING SAUCE FOR SALMON

This recipe will blow your mind!

4 8-ounce salmon fillets, with skins on

¼ cup hoisin sauce

1 tablespoon dark sesame oil

¼ teaspoon cayenne pepper

Mix together all ingredients to make sauce. Brush some of the sauce on the flesh side and then place the fillet on a hot grill, flesh side down, for about 2 minutes. Carefully turn it; then coat it with the sauce again and grill for 8 minutes more. It will come off the grill in one piece.

Makes enough for 4 (8-ounce) salmon fillets

SCALLOP CEVICHE

This easy ceviche has an unusual tropical flavor that's rich and light at the same time. The recipe calls for scallops, but it's also nice with conch, abalone, snapper, or even shrimp.

1¼ pounds sea scallops

⅓ cup freshly squeezed lemon juice

3 tablespoons freshly squeezed key lime juice

3 tablespoons freshly squeezed orange juice

2 teaspoons freshly grated ginger

2 serrano chiles, minced

Zest of 1 lime

½ bunch cilantro, chopped fine

½ cup chopped green onion

½ cup finely diced red bell pepper

2 cloves garlic, minced

3 tablespoons extra virgin olive oil

Dressing:

1 large ripe Hass avocado, chopped

1 Roma tomato, peeled, seeded, and chopped fine

1 tablespoon finely chopped cilantro

1 tablespoon finely chopped white onion

1 jalapeño chile, seeded and minced

1 clove garlic, minced

Juice of 1 key lime

Pinch of dark brown sugar

1½ tablespoons extra virgin olive oil

Salt and freshly ground black pepper to taste

Rinse the scallops under very cold water and dry with a paper towel. Cut the scallops in thirds creating short rounds. In a large nonreactive bowl mix together the lemon juice, lime juice, orange juice, ginger, serrano chiles, and lime zest. Mix well and then add the sliced scallops. Gently stir, then cover and refrigerate for 1 hour or until the scallops turn white. Add the cilantro, green onion, red bell pepper, garlic, and olive oil. Cover and refrigerate for 2 to 3 hours.

Gently fold all dressing ingredients together and then season to taste. Using a slotted spoon, divide the ceviche between 6 plates. Spoon the dressing over the ceviche and drizzle with a little of the ceviche marinade. Serve with ice-cold Mexican beer and fresh key limes.

Serves 6

SOY AND WASABI-BASTED SPINY-LOBSTER TACOS WITH CRUNCHY PEAR AND AVOCADO SALSA

If you cannot find the spiny lobster, any good quality lobster tails will do. This baste works well with any light grilled fish, but make sure to serve it with the Crunchy Pear and Avocado Salsa.

3 (8- to 10-ounce) spiny lobster tails

Crunchy Pear and Avocado Salsa:

2 medium pears, ripe but firm, chopped

2 red Fresno chiles with seeds, chopped

⅓ cup chopped white onion

⅓ cup chopped fresh cilantro

2 tablespoons finely chopped fresh mint

Juice of 2 key limes

1 teaspoon sugar

1 avocado, chopped

Soy and Wasabi Baste:

1 clove garlic, minced

1 stick sweet butter

2 tablespoons soy sauce

2 tablespoons wasabi powder

1½ tablespoons brown sugar, packed firm

Juice of 1 key lime

12 fresh corn tortillas

1 bunch spinach, julienned

Drop the lobster tails into lightly salted boiling water for exactly 3 minutes; immediately plunge them into a bowl of ice water to stop the cooking. Split the tails lengthwise with a French knife or heavy cleaver; they will still be a little raw in the center. Remove the dark vein running down the center of the tail. This first step can be done in advance, but keep the tails refrigerated until grill time.

For the Crunchy Pear and Avocado Salsa, mix together all salsa ingredients except the avocado, which should be gently folded in last. Set aside in the refrigerator, allowing flavors to blend.

For the Soy and Wasabi Baste, sauté the garlic in butter until golden. Remove from heat for 1 minute. Whisk in all other ingredients and simmer on low for 2 minutes, whisking constantly.

Lightly spray the flesh side of the lobster tails with nonstick vegetable oil spray. Spoon the warm baste over the flesh side of the lobster tails and then grill flesh side down over a medium hot grill for 2 1/2 minutes. Turn the tails and baste again, grilling the shell side for 2 1/2 minutes. Remove from grill, pull the lobster meat free from the shells, and then place the meat back in the shells. (This saves your guest a messy task.) Spoon a little more of the baste over the lobster meat. Serve on a big plate with a healthy dollop of Crunchy Pear and Avocado Salsa, a few warm corn tortillas, and some julienned spinach. Allow your guests to put the tacos together themselves.

Serves 6

SEARED AHI TUNA STEAKS

I've watched so many people try this for the first time. Usually they are a little squeamish about the center being raw. But after one bite they all say the same thing: "Wow! That is delicious!"

1 (6-ounce) #1 sushi-grade ahi tuna steak
   per person
Sesame oil
Salt and pepper

Brush both sides of the tuna with sesame oil and salt and pepper. Quickly sear each side over hot mesquite charcoal, about 1 to 1 1/2 minutes per side. Serve with Japanese soy sauce and wasabi.

PIQUANT BLACK PEPPER AND COGNAC SHRIMP APPETIZER

Spicy and elegant, this appetizer is the start of a perfect evening.

1 white onion, sliced thin
1½ tablespoons olive oil
Sea salt to taste
1 pound medium shrimp in their shells (this
   adds flavor to the sauce)
2 teaspoons black pepper
1 teaspoon crushed red chile
5 sprigs fresh thyme
⅓ cup cognac
6 tablespoons sweet butter, cut into chunks
1 tablespoon finely chopped fresh parsley
½ fresh lemon
Crusty French bread

Sauté the onion in the oil over medium-high heat until translucent. Season to taste with salt. Add the shrimp, black pepper, red chile and thyme. Sauté until shrimp are just cooked and have turned pink, about 2 minutes per side. Add cognac (be careful, as it can flare up), stir in the butter, and remove from heat. Add parsley and toss well; drizzle with lemon. Serve on a big platter. Everybody peels and eats while mopping up the sauce with the bread!

Serves 4

POBLANO QUINOA WITH GOAT CHEESE

I love to serve this with grill-roasted lamb chops. It's light and elegant!

1 celery stick, chopped

½ white onion, chopped

1 carrot, chopped

1 tablespoon extra virgin olive oil

1 cup quinoa, rinsed well

2 cups chicken broth or vegetable broth

½ cup pinyon nuts

1 roasted poblano chile, seeds removed and
   chopped

1 teaspoon Greek oregano

Salt and pepper to taste

3 ounces goat cheese, crumbled

In a medium saucepan, sauté the celery, onion, and carrot in the oil until soft, about 8 minutes. Add the quinoa, broth, pinyon nuts, poblano chile, oregano, salt, and pepper. Bring to a slow boil, cover, and reduce heat to low. Simmer until all moisture is absorbed, about 10 to 15 minutes. Remove from heat. Serve hot, topped with a little goat cheese.

Serves 5

THAI HOT SAUCE

Talk about good! If you're a salsa lover like me, this one will blow your mind. The flavors are definitely Asian, well-defined, complex, and very hot. Serve it over white rice with grilled fish, pork, or poultry.

6 cloves garlic

2 tablespoons chopped dried shrimp

4 dried chile de arbol

1½ teaspoons raw sugar

3 tablespoons fish sauce

3 tablespoons key lime juice

3 fresh Thai chiles, chopped fine

Combine the garlic, shrimp, chile de arbol, and sugar in a small food processor; grind into a course meal. Remove from food processor and add all other ingredients. Allow flavors to blend for 1 hour before serving. Keeps fresh in the refrigerator for several weeks.

Makes ¾ cup

HABANERO PAPAYA SALSA

If you've never tried fruited salsas, this is a good place to start.

1 habanero chile with seeds, chopped

1 cup papaya, pitted and cubed into
   ½-inch pieces

½ cup (½-inch cubes) red bell pepper

Juice of 1 large fresh lime

1 tablespoon golden raisins

1 tablespoon sun-dried tomato, packed in
   olive oil

1 tablespoon light olive oil

1 teaspoon minced fresh mint

1 teaspoon kosher salt

½ teaspoon black pepper

Mix all ingredients in a glass bowl; let chill for a few hours in the refriger-ator, covered in plastic wrap. Bring to room temperature before serving.

Make 2¼ cups

CHARRED PINEAPPLE SALSA

Grilled pineapple and chiles . . . you've simply got to try this. It's fantastic with anything off the grill. We pour it over grill-roasted chicken in the last twenty minutes of cooking. Talk about flavor!

3 (½-inch) slices fresh pineapple, core
   removed

2 poblano chiles

½ red bell pepper

1 jalapeño

2 (½-inch) slices white onion

Grill all ingredients until charred brown and soft. Place poblano and red bell pepper in a plastic bag and twist closed, removing as much air as is possible. Allow chiles and red bell pepper to steam in their own heat for about 10 minutes. Remove from plastic bag; skin should come off easily. Remove stems and seeds from chiles and bell pepper. Chop all ingredients. Place in a medium-size mixing bowl. Let stand for 30 minutes to blend for flavors.

Makes 2 cups

"It is my opinion that California can and does furnish the best bad things that America has to offer." Hinton Helper (1881), author of *Life in California.*

GRILLED LOBSTER SALSA

We use this salsa with grill-roasted lobster, but it goes well with any grilled seafood!

3 large ripe Roma tomatoes, cut into ½-inch
  chunks

½ English cucumber, peeled and cut into
  ½-inch chunks

2 teaspoons salt

Pepper to taste

3 serrano chiles, chopped fine

½ white onion, chopped fine

1 bunch cilantro, cleaned and chopped

4 large Hass avocados, cut into ¾-inch
  chunks

Place the tomatoes and cucumber in a large bowl and season with the salt and pepper; let macerate for 10 to 15 minutes. Add all other ingredients except avocado and mix well; then fold in avocado. Blend for about 1 hour before serving.

Makes 3 cups

CUCUMBER DILL SALSA FOR GRILLED FISH

Yes, the last salsa recipe in the book omits chile, but there's something about the combination of cucumber, dill, and grilled fish. Besides, you can always chomp on a habanero while enjoying this!

2 medium tomatoes, seeded, peeled, and
  chopped

1 cup chopped English cucumber

1 tablespoon finely chopped fresh dill

1 teaspoon salt

Mix all ingredients together. Let flavors blend for 1 hour.

Makes 2 cups

While filming *Cleopatra*, American actress Elizabeth Taylor supposedly paid $200, quite a sum at that time, to have ten quarts of Chasen's famous chili flown to her in Rome.

ASIAN MACADAMIA-NUT PEACH ROLLS

You can make these rolls with whatever fruit is in season. Try combinations like banana or strawberry with pecan, or apple with walnut. Cut them on an angle at different lengths, stand them cut side up on a platter, drizzle with the syrup, and dust them with powdered sugar. We set out the platter with hot coffee and they just disappear!

1 fresh peach

1 tablespoon granulated sugar

¼ cup crushed Macadamia nuts

2 tablespoons brown sugar

½ teaspoons ground cinnamon

8 egg-roll wrappers

1 egg white mixed with ¼ cup water

Oil for frying

Confectioners' sugar

Brown Sugar Cinnamon Syrup (see below)

Peel the peach, remove the pit, and chop into ½-inch cubes. Mix the chopped peach with the granulated sugar. Set aside for 20 minutes.

Mix together the nuts, brown sugar, and cinnamon. Lay an egg-roll wrapper on a clean surface. Make a line 1 inch up from the bottom that stops 1 inch in from both sides. Spoon 2 tablespoons of the nut mixture and 2 tablespoons of the chopped peaches into this marked area. Brush a line up the sides of the wrapper and fold a 1-inch flap to cover some of the filling on both sides. Now brush a 2-inch line across the top of the wrapper and, starting at the bottom of the wrapper, roll up the filling, creating a little fruit egg roll. Deep-fry the rolls in 375-degree oil until deep brown. Drain on paper towels. Cut in half, dust with confectioners' sugar, and serve with warm Brown Sugar Cinnamon Syrup.

Makes 8 servings

BROWN SUGAR CINNAMON SYRUP

This syrup is for the Asian Macadamia-Nut Peach Rolls (see above). But it also goes very well as a dessert topping for ice cream, baked goods, or sopapillas. We even use it on waffles.

1 cup brown sugar

1 cup water

1 cinnamon stick

In a small saucepan dissolve the brown sugar in the water, add the cinnamon stick, and bring to a boil over medium heat; reduce until thick.

Makes 1½ cups

INDEX